Provided
by

Measure B

which was approved
by the voters in
November, 1998

LITTLE PEOPLE

and a

LOST WORLD

AN ANTHROPOLOGICAL MYSTERY

LITTLE PEOPLE

and a

LOST WORLD

AN ANTHROPOLOGICAL MYSTERY

LINDA GOLDENBERG

TWENTY-FIRST CENTURY BOOKS · MINNEAPOLIS

Title page photo: *Scientists carefully brush the soil from ancient bones discovered on Flores Island, Indonesia, in 2003.*

Twenty-First Century Books
A division of Lerner Publishing Group
241 First Avenue North
Minneapolis, Minnesota 55401 U.S.A.

Website address: www.lernerbooks.com

Library of Congress Cataloging-in-Publication Data

Goldenberg , Linda.
    Little people and a lost world : an anthropological mystery / by Linda Goldenberg.
        p.   cm. — (Discovery!)
    Includes bibliographical references and index.
    ISBN-13: 978-0-8225-5983-2 (lib. bdg. : alk. paper)
    ISBN-10: 0-8225-5983-8 (lib. bdg. : alk. paper)
    1. Fossil hominids—Indonesia—Flores Island. 2. Pygmies—Indonesia—Flores Island.
3. Excavations (Archaeology)—Indonesia—Flores Island. 4. Human remains
(Archaeology)—Indonesia—Flores Island. 5. Flores Island (Indonesia)—Antiquities.
    I. Title. II. Series: Discovery! (Lerner Publishing Group)
    GN730.32.I5A85 2007
    569.909598'6—dc22   2005033431

Manufactured in the United States of America
1 2 3 4 5 6 – BP – 12 11 10 09 08 07

CONTENTS

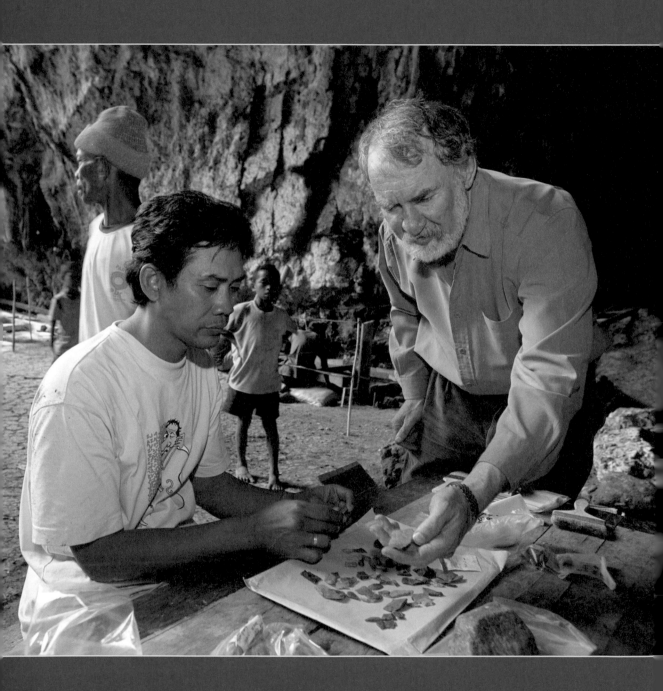

CHAPTER ONE

THE LITTLE PEOPLE ARE DISCOVERED

It was mid-September 2003, almost the rainy season on Flores Island, one of the small, rugged islands of southern Indonesia known as the Lesser Sunda Islands. A team of scientists had been at work since June, excavating a cave in the western highlands. Now it was time to go home.

The team—archaeologists, anthropologists, and other specialists—had been looking for ancient human remains. Such evidence would verify their belief that an early human species, *Homo erectus*, known to have lived on nearby Java, had also lived on Flores Island in the far distant past. Most people thought it would not have been possible for them to reach the island. But the team had reason to believe they had. One of the organizers of the dig, archaeologist Michael Morwood of the University of New England, Australia, had uncovered, on an expedition several years earlier, what he thought were tools more than eight hundred thousand years old. Now the scientists were searching for remains of their makers.

(AN AMAZING FIND

The team was a partnership of Australians and Indonesians, but the Australians had already left. Their three-month visas

Mike Morwood (right) and Wahyu Saptomo look through finds from the Liang Bua cave on Flores Island.

Paleontologist Thomas Sutikna (left) *and members of his crew found fossil bones while digging in Liang Bua cave in 2003.*

(permits to work in the country) had expired at the end of August. Within a few days, before the rains began, the Indonesians would disband the work crew and go home themselves.

This was the researchers' third year at the cave. They had excavated several other sites on the island, but beginning in the dry season of 2001, they had concentrated on Liang Bua—which means "cool cave" in the local language. It was an especially promising site because the soil on the cave floor was very deep and no one had ever dug to the bottom. This year they had reached a level 20 feet (6 meters) below the surface. They had carefully brushed away the earth, carrying it out of the shaft in buckets, examining it for any signs of human presence—bones or artifacts. Next year they would dig deeper.

And then, brushing once more through the earth closest to the left wall, workers saw what looked like a slice of bone.

Everyone gathered in silence. A few more careful sweeps and they saw a human skull. Then a jawbone emerged, and then a pelvic (hip) bone and a set of leg bones—almost an entire skeleton.

Since the skeleton was barely 3 feet (1 m) tall, they assumed it was that of a child. But child or not, it was what they had been looking for. These were ancient human remains, stunning proof that they had been on the right track.

Paleontologist Thomas Sutikna of the Indonesian Centre for Archaeology was in charge that day. He realized immediately that the remains were too fragile to be moved or even touched. They had not fossilized. They had not turned into stone, but had the consistency, he later said, of "mashed potatoes." They would have to be allowed to air dry before anything more could be done.

Paleontologist Thomas Sutikna inspects the parts of a female skeleton that were found in Liang Bua in 2003.

IT TAKES A TEAM

Scientists from several fields and specialties work at excavations. "Our team [at Flores Island] had everyone involved," said Bert Roberts, a senior researcher at the University of Wollongong, Australia. "Geomorphologists, geochronologists, archaeologists, paleoanthropologists—Good grief, it was a soccer team of [scientists]."

In the past, a researcher might go into the field alone and return with experts as they were needed. But in the twenty-first century, it is understood that a group effort is needed from the beginning. Here are a few of the sciences that contribute. The boundaries between them sometimes overlap.

Paleoanthropology is the study of human origins and development, based primarily on fossils. It combines parts of two other sciences: **paleontology**, the study of ancient life of all kinds, and **anthropology**, the study of the origin and development of human beings and societies.

Archaeology is the study of prehistoric human life based on artifacts (things made by human beings) such as the stone tools found in the cave at Liang Bua.

Geochronology and **geomorphology** are specialties within the science of **geology,** the study of the earth. Geochronologists study the age of rocks and sediments. This helps determine the age of fossils and artifacts found with them. Geomorphologists study the origin and development of landforms. At excavations these specialists often work closely with **palynologists**, who study fossil pollen (the powdery substance that fertilizes flowers). They try to determine what kinds of plants lived during the prehistoric past and when they lived.

Paleo means "old." Many sciences have paleo-versions. **Paleobotany**, for example, is the study of ancient plant life. Palynology is a specialty within paleobotany. **Paleoecology** is the study of ancient environments. **Paleoclimatology** is the study of ancient climates. More specialties will probably be named in the future, as finer scientific tools and methods are developed.

All work stopped. No one was sure of what they had found, but it was already incredible—almost an entire prehistoric human skeleton 20 feet (6 m) beneath the surface of Liang Bua.

When Sutikna determined that the remains were sufficiently dry, he supervised the application of a commercial glue, which acted as a hardening agent. Paleontologist Rukus Awe Due was able to closely observe the skeleton's teeth. He saw that they were very worn and the third molars had come in. This meant that the person had not been a child but an adult at least twenty years old, which puzzled everyone. But nothing more could be determined until they got the little skeleton to the laboratory. The bones, together with the surrounding earth, were lifted from the cave floor in blocks. These were carefully packed and carried to the dirt road above. "We cradled them in our arms," Sutikna recalled.

It was only a distance of about 10 miles (16 kilometers) to the nearest village, Ruteng, but it took them an hour to reach it on the rough dirt road, which was little more than a trail. There they picked up the main road and began the four-hour drive through the mountains to the small airport on the coast. They boarded a plane and, holding the remains on their laps, Sutikna and the others flew to Jakarta, the capital of Indonesia.

Peter Brown, an Australian anthropologist and senior member of the team, had already been contacted by the crew and was waiting for them when they arrived. The remains were carefully unpacked and laid out in the laboratory for examination. "I would have been less surprised if someone had uncovered an alien," Brown said.

DATING METHODS

Until the 1950s, scientists had no way of knowing exactly when in the prehistoric past an event had occurred. They could only date things relative to one another—which came before and which came after. Archaeologists, for example, knew that stone tools were in use before metal tools, and that, of the metals, bronze was in use before iron. They called the period when stone tools were used the Stone Age. They knew that it came first, the Bronze Age second, and the Iron Age last. But they did not know when these periods were—whether the Stone Age took place eight or eighty thousand years ago.

This changed in the 1950s, when scientists developed methods that could determine exactly how old something was. The techniques were based on research from World War II (1939–1945) into atomic energy and radioactivity. They are called radiometric techniques. They determine the age of something by measuring radioactive decay, the time it takes for a radioactive material to change into a stable, nonradioactive material.

Radiocarbon dating was the first of these new techniques. It is based on the fact that all living plants and animals constantly absorb radioactive carbon, also called carbon 14. When a plant or animal dies, it stops absorbing carbon. The radioactive carbon in the plant or animal decays and turns into nonradioactive carbon. Because it does this at a known rate, scientists can determine when any organic material died—bones, plants, wood, and anything made from them.

Radiocarbon dating was revolutionary when it was developed, but it is accurate for measurements only up to about fifty thousand years. Soon other radiometric techniques were developed that could determine the age of even older objects. **Electron spin resonance dating** is based on the damage that naturally occurs in minerals due to exposure to radiation. It is used to determine the approximate age of fossilized teeth and shells. It can date things up to two million years old.

Several other methods are in use. **Uranium series dating** is a group of techniques based on the radioactive decay of some forms of uranium. **Optically stimulated luminescence dating (OSL)** is one of the newest methods. It is used to determine when inorganic materials such as minerals were last exposed to sunlight.

For scientists to accept a date as correct, it must be confirmed by more than one dating method. The more results that agree, the more likely it is that the date is accurate.

The development of radiometric techniques revolutionized the study of the prehistoric past. It showed that human beings and Earth itself were much older than had ever been imagined.

Radiocarbon dating of charcoal fragments found next to the skeleton showed that it was about eighteen thousand years old. Examination of the pelvic bone showed it to be a female. Growth lines on the skull confirmed what Due had noticed when he looked at her teeth. The skeleton was not that of a child but an adult about thirty years old when she died. Brown determined that the volume of her brain was about 23 cubic inches (380 cubic centimeters), smaller than the brain of a chimpanzee. She would have weighed about 30 pounds (14 kilograms) and stood just 3 feet (almost 1 m) tall. "Hominids [human ancestors] of that size were supposed to have become extinct three million years ago," Brown said. "My jaw dropped to my knees."

(LOOKING FOR MORE BONES

Could this little person have been an anomaly, a single oddity? Perhaps the scientists had happened upon the remains of someone whose growth had been stunted by disease. More remains would have to be found before they could know.

Over the next year, during the dry season, the excavation continued and more remains were indeed unearthed. The team found the arm bones of the first little skeleton, a second jawbone, and fragments of what were thought to be seven more individuals. Of those whose heights could be determined, none had been more than 3 feet (almost 1 m) tall.

Remains of animals had also been found in the cave. Among them were stegodons, an early species of elephant now extinct. Mainland stegodons had weighed several tons, but these had been dwarfs, about the size of ponies, and had weighed about 1 ton (almost 1 metric ton).

Workers carry buckets of earth excavated from Liang Bua cave to a wash station located in a nearby rice paddy. Each load of earth is carefully washed and sifted through to find any traces of human or animal remains.

The bones of enormous rats and giant monitor lizards, including a Komodo dragon, were found as well. Komodo dragons today weigh about 500 pounds (more than 200 kilograms). This one would have weighed hundreds of pounds more.

Bert Roberts assisted by Kira Westaway and Chris Turney, worked to establish the age of the finds. In addition to radiocarbon dating, three other methods were used on the tooth enamel of a young stegodon found near one set of remains.

These methods were luminescence dating, which determines when something was last exposed to sunlight; uranium-series dating of flowstone, the crystals of calcite that are deposited in caves by dripping water; and electron-spin resonance dating. The results of all four methods agreed with one another. They showed that the small creatures had occupied the cave from about ninety-five thousand until about thirteen thousand years ago. The dig at Liang Bua had uncovered something amazing: little people and a lost world.

Dwarf stegadon teeth (right) *were found in Liang Bua, as well as stone tools and little people bones.*

The huge entrance to Liang Bua dwarfs scientists and other workers.

(THE LITTLE PEOPLE

No one knows how many of the little people there were or exactly what they looked like, but they made use of Liang Bua for more than eighty thousand years. Tucked into the side of a mountain, fronted by a broad rocky ledge, the cave is an enormous 13,000 square feet (1,200 sq. m). With its dropped floor and arched ceilings, it is as high as a two-story house, always cool and often flooded with sunlight. Morwood compared it to a cathedral. The little people made fires there, worked on the tools they needed for hunting and cooking, and found shelter from the weather and perhaps protection from the animals.

Like other early humans, the people of Liang Bua were hunter-gatherers. They ate the wild plants they could find and the animals they could catch, trap, or hunt. Komodo dragons would have been their worst enemy and, if they hunted them, a great catch, but it can't be determined whether the dragon bones in the cave are the bones of a killer or a victim.

Komodo dragons hunt by ambush. They can run quickly only for very short distances, not more than 50 feet (15 m). Then they collapse, exhausted. So they lie in wait for their prey. When prey comes within striking range, they race out, club it with their tail, and bite it with their razor-sharp teeth. Sometimes they take down their prey on the spot. But even if they

Two Komodo dragons patrol the beach on an Indonesian island.

don't, the bitten creature is doomed. Within hours it will be unable to move, and within a day, it will die. It had been thought that the rotting meat in a dragon's mouth left from its last meal in combination with its saliva, which contains deadly germs, makes its bite deadly. New research points to the animal's own venom. Either way, the dragon's bite kills its prey.

A Komodo dragon's favorite leisure activity is dozing and basking in the sun, which would give hunters the opportunity to take it by surprise. Or, knowing the dragon's weakness, hunters could have attracted its attention, made it run, and killed it when it collapsed.

Though the scientists can't be sure that the dragon in the cave had been the victim of a hunt, other animal bones tell a clear story. Stegodons were not carnivorous (meat-eating) and were not good climbers. They would not have gone to the cave on their own. They had to have been brought there. And some of their bones were charred, as if they had been roasted over a fire. Some had cut marks on them.

Most of the stegodon bones are those of babies, who might have been just the right size for hunters no bigger than modern-day three-year-old children themselves. But some were of adults. And though, at 1 ton (almost 1 metric ton), they were much smaller than adult stegodons on the mainland, they would still have been a great challenge to the little hunters. Their weapons were spears, delicate stone barbs and points, like arrowheads, attached to sticks. It must have taken a good number of these tiny spears to fell even a small-size stegodon.

The little people made the barbs and points by chipping away at one stone with another until they had the shape, size, and sharpness they wanted. They were excellent stoneworkers.

Delicate stone points, or arrowheads, and other stone tools were found in Liang Bua.

Many other finely made tools were also found in the cave. Some seem designed for scraping, others for chopping, and some, with blade-sharp edges, for cutting.

Because the little people seem to have done things together—they hunted, made fires, and cooked—Morwood and others believe that the little people of Flores, or Floresiens, had language. Roberts says their group activities suggest that they had at least "a functional level of communication." But many animals—wolves, lions, and others—work together without structured language. Even the ability to make cooking fires is not considered proof that the little people could speak. Things that would be considered proof—artwork, for example, and ornaments, which show the ability to use symbols—have not been found in the cave.

Unclear also is exactly what the Floresiens looked like. Soft tissue, such as skin, decays without leaving remains that scientists can analyze. There is no way to know the color of their skin or eyes, the size of their noses or ears, the color or texture of their hair. Their arms were longer than today's humans compared to the rest of their bodies, though no one is sure what that might mean. Perhaps long arms enabled them to find safety and lookouts in trees. "We don't know this," said paleontologist Chris Stringer, director of the Department of Human Origins at the Natural History Museum, London. Peter Brown had kept him informed of the investigation, and Stringer was often asked for his opinion. "But if there were Komodo dragons about, you might want to be up in the trees with your babies." Brown, on the other hand, noting the first little skeleton's delicate hand and wrist bones, said she would have made a wonderful watchmaker, but he suspected that "she wasn't doing a lot of climbing." Like all hunter-gatherers, the little people probably spent most of their time searching for food and staying out of harm's way.

(FLORES ISLAND

Flores and the other Lesser Sunda Islands lie to the east of the Indonesian island of Java. The area is on a "hot spot," a place where there are frequent volcanic eruptions and earthquakes.

Flores itself was created by volcanic activity on the ocean floor. It rose above sea level as an island of lava and volcanic debris more than one million years ago, and it has been the scene of violent geologic disturbances ever since. The island has fourteen active volcanoes, and four exploded in major eruptions during the twentieth century. The most destructive of these eruptions occurred in 1992 and killed more than two thousand people.

Twelve thousand years ago, the island was rocked by a particularly violent string of volcanic explosions that continued for many months. Geologists know this because of the changes the explosions created in the landscape and the lava they left behind. Liang Bua survived the disturbances, but it

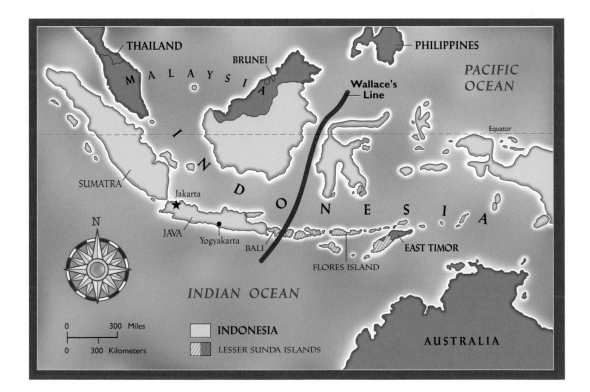

The volcanic islands of the Lesser Sundas rise sharply from the ocean. The area is still regularly rocked by volcanic activity and earthquakes.

was never again used by the little people. Perhaps they abandoned the cave for another site that has not yet been located. Perhaps they left the island altogether. Most people think they were all killed, but no one can be sure. "One of the interesting things about my subject [paleoanthropology]," Brown said in an interview, "is that it's only as good as the next discovery."

(TELLING THE WORLD

In October 2004, the Liang Bua finds were made public in *Nature*, one of the world's most highly respected scientific journals. *Nature* publishes articles only after they have been reviewed by a panel of experts. Most of the articles are specialized and are not of interest to the general public. But after the October issue of *Nature* came out, the discovery was headlined in magazines and newspapers around the world. The scientists named the little species *Homo floresiensis* (person of Flores), but the press called them hobbits—Morwood's nickname for

Nature *magazine broke the story about* Homo floresiensis. *Professor Chris Stringer* (right) *and the editor of* Nature *magazine, Henry Gee, appeared at a news conference in London with casts of* Homo erectus (left), Homo floresiensis (center), *and* Homo sapiens (right), *or modern human, skulls.*

them—after the fictional race of tiny people in J. R. R. Tolkien's popular *Lord of the Rings* trilogy. When Roberts told an interviewer that he had been "gobsmacked" by the discovery, he didn't have to explain what he meant. A British newspaper, the *Guardian*, said the discovery "challenges the history of evolution." And the *Guardian*'s featured columnist, David Aaronovitch, wrote that at first he thought the discovery was "some kind of Aussie [Australian] hoax," because "it seemed to be too good a story—too fabulous, too interesting, too uplifting . . . to be really true."

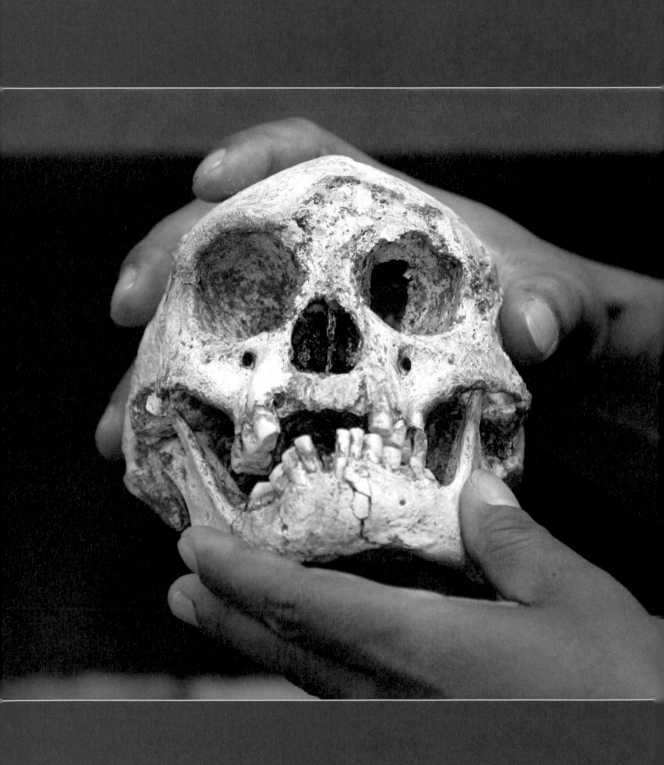

CHAPTER TWO

PUZZLES AND WONDERS

Aaronovitch wrote that the scientists who discovered the tiny creatures were "in love with their find" and so were people everywhere. But very little about the Floresiens could be understood.

Their ancestry, for one thing, could not be determined. The only hominids that had ever been as small were the little prehumans called australopithecines. Some scientists think australopithecines were direct ancestors of *Homo sapiens*, but others think they were more like cousins. The most complete and most famous australopithecine ever discovered, nicknamed Lucy, had been an adult female, 3 feet 8 inches (a little more than 1 m) tall. But she had lived three and a half million years ago in Ethiopia. All australopithecines, it was believed, had become extinct without ever leaving Africa.

Homo erectus, the first human species known to have migrated out of Africa, had been in the Indonesian islands at the right time. These were the early humans whose remains the scientists had hoped to find. But *Homo erectus* had been the size of modern humans and, judging by their tools, not nearly as intelligent as *Homo floresiensis*. In addition, *Homo erectus* had never been known to cross the open sea, and scientists believed that they were incapable of doing so. *Homo sapiens* did cross

An Indonesian scientist holds one of the mysterious skulls found in Liang Bua.

the sea and made tools similar to those found on Flores, but by the time *Homo sapiens* left Africa and settled in the islands, the little people had been living on Flores for forty thousand years.

(THE ISLAND RULE

Who the Floresiens were and where they came from were mysteries, but scientists could offer a possible explanation for their size. Giant and dwarf versions of animals had long been found on isolated islands. Madagascar, off the coast of Africa in the Indian Ocean, has giant cockroaches. The Seychelles, a sprinkling of tiny islands north of Madagascar, has ant-sized frogs. The island of Jersey, off the northern coast of France, had tiny red-tail deer. Santa Rosa, 50 miles (80 km) off the coast of

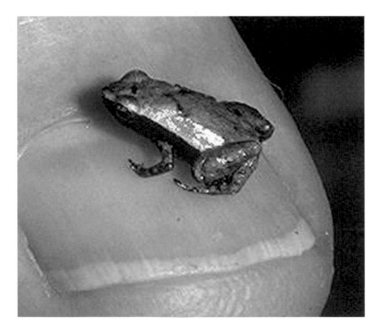

A tiny Gardiner's tree frog from the Seychelles island group is smaller than a fingernail.

California, once had small mammoths, and in the Mediterranean Sea, the island of Cyprus had hippopotamuses the size of pigs. The unusual sizes of animals on islands had been studied in the 1960s by biologist J. Bristol Foster. He studied 116 different species, including rabbits, rodents, deer, and hippopotamuses, that lived on islands along the coasts of western North America and Europe. He then compared them with their mainland counterparts. The conclusion he drew came to be known as the island rule. It states that over time, large mammals on isolated islands tend to become smaller and small mammals tend to become larger.

According to Foster, the absence of predators is the reason for both kinds of change. Without natural enemies, he explained, small animals can safely become larger and therefore tend to do so. Large animals, on the other hand, without natural enemies to keep their numbers low, soon overwhelm the food supply. They can survive only if they become smaller. This easily accounted for the small elephants and giant rats and lizards on Flores. It was difficult to believe that a human species would also follow this rule—there were no known examples of it anywhere in the world—but it was a possible explanation.

There was no explanation at all, however, for their small brains in combination with what seemed intelligence. Until this discovery, it was considered a fact that intelligence and brain size go together. Most descriptions of the human species begin by explaining that our large brain is our distinguishing difference and makes our great intelligence possible. But the Floresiens had tiny brains even in proportion to their bodies. Their brains were smaller than the brains of chimpanzees, one-third the size of an adult human brain, half the size of the brain of a newborn baby. And judging from the tools found with them, they had been very intelligent. This should not have been possible and could not be explained at all.

Brown would have liked to make a mold of the tiny skull, but he determined that it was too fragile. Instead, he arranged to have CT scans taken of the skull's interior. These scans use computers to translate waves of energy hitting a solid object into a three-dimensional image of the object. He hoped that these scans would help him understand more about the little brain the skull had once held. He found the Floresiens' small stature easy enough to understand. "But small brain size was a bigger problem," he said. "It still is."

Scientists have always supposed that intelligence increased with larger brain size. The Flores Island find calls this into question.

(WALLACE'S LINE

It was also hard to explain the little people's presence on Flores Island. According to everything that was known about Earth's history and human migration, they should not have been able to get there. Flores lies east of what is called Wallace's Line, an imaginary line suggested by Alfred Russel Wallace in the 1850s. A self-taught English naturalist, Wallace lived on the Indonesian island of Sumatra for several years. Like Charles Darwin in England, he was trying to understand how species change over

Alfred Russel Wallace, who lived on Sumatra for many years, discovered that the fossils on some of the islands resembled those on the mainland, and on other islands, they were very different.

time. He sailed to almost all the islands in the area collecting fossils. Some islands, he found, had been home to all the animals that could be found on the mainland. Others had been home to hardly any. The line he proposed divides the two groups. It follows an underwater trench so deep—1,100 feet (335 m)—that even during ice ages, when sea levels fell by 490 feet (149 m) and many parts of the ocean disappeared completely, deep waters remained along this corridor.

During the ice ages, the islands west of the line—Bali, Java, and Sumatra—had been connected to one another and to the continent by land bridges. But the islands east of it, such as Flores, had always been separated by deep water and treacherous currents. The only mammals to reach them had been rodents, who could have been washed there on debris, and stegodons, which were so buoyant that they could have swum and floated there on their own. Now it seemed a human species, well before *Homo sapiens*, had also reached an island east of Wallace's Line.

They couldn't have swum there, but perhaps they had arrived accidentally, carried by the currents on logs or vegetation that had fallen into the sea during a storm. This theory had once been suggested to explain how the first people reached Australia. It had seemed unlikely when it was proposed, but it became more believable after the Indian Ocean tsunami of 2005, when many people were rescued after floating on logs and other debris for days and, in some cases, weeks. Nevertheless, Morwood believed it was more likely that the first people to reach Flores had arrived on watercraft they made themselves. If they had been able to reach the island accidentally on natural rafts tossed ashore by the currents, surely other large mammals—pigs, deer, monkeys, tigers—would have reached it that way as well. But they didn't.

The only mammal fossils found on Flores aside from rodents and stegodons were those of the little humans. "The most likely explanation," Chris Stringer said, "as difficult as it is for me to accept, is that they used some kind of watercraft."

As strange as their arrival was the fact that they had lived on the island as recently as thirteen thousand years ago. This was long after *Homo sapiens*, modern human beings, had arrived on many nearby islands and even on Australia. It was also thousands of years after modern humans were thought to be the only human species on Earth. In fact, modern humans had lived in the same region as these little humans for at least thirty thousand years. The two groups might even have met. Yet before the remains of the little Floresiens were found, scientists would have said there had never been such creatures.

It was obvious that many scientific theories would have to be revised and some ideas discarded entirely. The puzzle of the Floresiens' ancestry, their arrival on Flores Island, and the wonders of their size, their intelligence, and their relatively recent coexistence with modern human beings—everything about them made the little people a big story and perhaps the greatest scientific mystery of our time. One paleoanthropologist called the discovery "a total knockout."

CHAPTER THREE

FINDING FLORES

The little people could easily have gone undiscovered. "I am superstitious and believe in luck," said one of the world's leading paleoanthropologists, Donald Johanson, in the book he wrote about his own work, *Lucy: The Beginnings of Humankind*. "Most of us are, because the work we do depends a great deal on luck. The fossils we study are extremely rare, and quite a few distinguished paleoanthropologists have gone a lifetime without finding a single one." The road that led scientists to a remote, largely unknown Indonesian island and the find of the century is as full of odd twists, unusual people, and incredible good luck as any could ever be.

Although people have always wondered about the origin and development of the human race, the subject was not studied scientifically until the nineteenth century. Until then, most people believed that the earth was only a few thousand years old and that life on Earth had always been the same. People found fossil bones, but no one knew where they came from.

In the mid-1800s, heavy humanlike bones were found in the Neander Valley of Germany and elsewhere in Europe. They turned out to belong to Neanderthals, a fairly recent human relative.

There was no way of knowing how old Earth was, when human life began, or how it began.

In 1858 fossil remains were found in a cave in the Neander Valley in Germany. The bones were strange, different from our own in some ways—they were very heavy, there was a thick ridge over the eye sockets, and the jaw was oddly set back—but they were clearly human. The miners who happened upon them thought they might be the bones of someone who had been murdered. They turned them over to a local police detective, who gave them to a science teacher to examine.

Today we know that these fossils are at least one hundred thousand years old. They are the remains of a prehistoric human relative, called *Homo neanderthalis*, or Neanderthal, now extinct. But at the time of their discovery, the leading scientists in Europe, who eventually examined them, did not understand what they were. To explain their peculiarities, some said they were the remains of a deformed human being. Others said that they might be the remains of a soldier who had hidden in the cave during the wars of the previous century. Europe's most famous expert in anatomy believed that they were the remains of someone who had had rickets (a bone disease) as a child and arthritis (a joint disease) as an old man and had been beaten on the head as a youth.

By this time, however, naturalists—as people who studied the natural world were called—had carefully observed living plants and small animals. They saw that living things change over the course of generations. And just as the Neander Valley discoveries were being discussed, Charles Darwin, the greatest naturalist of all, published his book, *The Origin of Species*, and formally introduced the theory of natural selection. He proposed that all living species had evolved from earlier forms. Although he did not deal with human beings in his first and

This drawing, showing some of the stages in human development from apes, attempts to illustrate Darwin's theory of evolution. From left to right, they are an African ape, an Australopithecus afarensis, *a* Homo habilis, *a* Homo erectus, *a* Homo neanderthalis, *and a modern human.*

most famous book, he suggested at the end of it that they too, like all other species, had developed over time.

This idea was very controversial. Most people believed that human beings had always been as they were, a unique creation. They found the idea that humans had developed over time, just as other creatures had, ridiculous or disturbing. Even most scientists at the time did not connect this idea with the bones found in the Neander Valley or think they might be the remains of an early kind of human being. But in the decades that followed, some scientists made the connection. Among them was Eugene Dubois, and the path to Flores begins with him.

(THE QUEST OF EUGENE DUBOIS

Dubois was Dutch. He was a medical doctor, a professor of anatomy, and a determined, independent scientist. The Neanderthal bones were discovered shortly before he was born, and he grew up fascinated by the discussions about them. As an adult in the 1880s, after studying the views of Darwin, he became convinced that the Neanderthal bones were the remains of an early human and that other, still earlier forms could be found.

Most young Darwinists, scientists researching Darwin's ideas, followed a suggestion Darwin made in a later book, *The Descent of Man*, and believed that human beings had originated in Africa. Others thought humans arose in Europe. Because of the large population of apes on the islands of Southeast Asia, one well-known scientist thought the human race had begun there.

Dubois, too, was impressed with the great number of apes and monkeys that coexisted with human beings on the Southeast Asian islands. He came to believe that this was the place to look for the creature that might have been the missing link, the early species that linked humans with apes.

Dubois had no evidence to support his belief. It was a hunch that his colleagues and family urged him not to follow. But in the late 1880s, he volunteered to be a military doctor and asked for an assignment in the islands of what was then the Dutch East Indies.

Dubois was stationed first on the island of Sumatra, where he conducted excavations in his spare time. When he contracted malaria, he was sent on medical leave to Java. There, in 1891, as he was exploring along the banks of a river, he made two finds not far from each other: the top of a skull and a leg bone. The skull was too heavy to be that of a man, and it was too large to be that of an ape. The leg bone was that of a creature that had walked upright. Dubois believed he had found what he had been searching for—remains of an intermediate creature between apes and humans.

Dubois crated the bones and took them back to Europe, but instead of acclaim, he was met with disbelief. Some scientists thought that he had found the remains of two different creatures, the skull of an ape and the leg bone of a human being. Others thought that he had found the remains not of a missing link but of a deformed person. Dubois became so furious at the

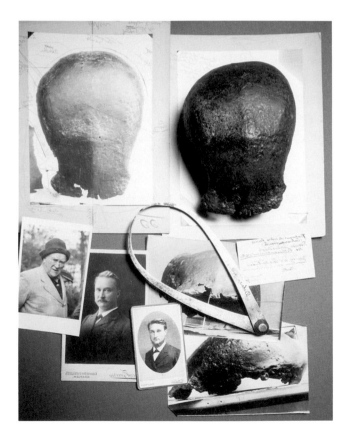

This composite photo shows Eugene Dubois, along with images of the fossil skull he found digging on Java.

This skullcap was found by Ralph von Koenigswald in Java in 1938. It belonged to the human relative Homo erectus.

scientists and their opinions that he stopped allowing people to examine the bones. Finally, he buried them under his dining room floor. But fifty years later, the story of his discovery would be an inspiration to another Dutchman, Theodor Verhoeven.

(THEODOR VERHOEVEN'S STONE TOOLS

Verhoeven was not a scientist by training. He was a priest, a missionary, and a self-taught archaeologist. He was delighted to serve in the islands of Southeast Asia for many reasons, including his knowledge of Dubois' find on Java in 1891. Those remains finally had been confirmed as being at least five hundred thousand years old. And in the 1930s, another researcher had found more skull fragments along the same riverbank.

Verhoeven lived on Flores Island during the 1950s and 1960s. He understood that, unlike Java, Flores was east of Wallace's Line, so he did not expect to find remains as old as those Dubois had found. But he hoped to find something of interest, and he excavated likely sites whenever he could. He visited Liang Bua many times, and once he brought a group of students to see it. "He would walk around wondering what was under his feet," an Australian archaeologist was later told.

Verhoeven did not find anything at Liang Bua, but at another site in the valley nearby, he did. He discovered stone tools near the bones of stegodons that were known to be about eight hundred thousand years old. He thought the tools must be the same age as the bones. He published his findings, but they were not taken seriously. Scientists at the time considered it impossible for humans of any kind to have reached an island east of Wallace's Line at such an early date. Since Verhoeven was an amateur and his findings so unlikely to be true, they were dismissed. The dating methods that would soon revolutionize paleoanthropology were just beginning to be developed, but no one even considered using them on the "improbable" finds of an unknown priest.

Several digs were conducted on Flores in the 1970s and 1980s. One team, led by distinguished Indonesian archaeologist Radien P. Soejono, excavated the floor of Liang Bua itself. But because of financial difficulties, the team was not able to excavate all the way to the bottom, and they did not find anything. Verhoeven's claims continued to be largely ignored. Flores Island remained what it had always been: a rugged, little-known island, beautiful but difficult to get to, of interest only to the people who lived there.

(A NEW TEAM EXCAVATES

And then in the early 1990s, archaeologist Michael Morwood came upon Verhoeven's papers. Morwood was studying the migrations of people through the Indonesian islands and Australia. He and colleague Douglas Hobbs had been excavating in the Kimberley region on Australia's west coast. They knew that seventeenth- and eighteenth-century seafarers, sailing south from Indonesia, had regularly landed there. They wondered whether the first people to reach the Australian continent had used the same currents. They wanted to explore these, beginning with the waters just north of Australia. "So we hired a boat and went sailing," Hobbs recalled, "in the shallow Arafura Sea."

They studied the routes between Australia and the closest Indonesian islands. One of them was Flores. Morwood knew that Verhoeven's claims had not been accepted at the time they were made, but the possibility that they had been correct was too intriguing to ignore. He wanted to take another look.

Since Flores is an Indonesian island, he needed to get permission from the Indonesian government to work there. And he would need the help and support of Indonesian scientists, many of whom had a great deal of experience in their fossil-rich nation. He contacted the Indonesian Geological Research and Development Centre. Scientists there were enthusiastic about the project. In 1995, along with Hobbs and other colleagues, Morwood headed to Flores.

The researchers began excavations in the Soa Basin. This was the wide valley used as grazing land for cattle and water buffalo, where Verhoeven made his finds in the 1960s. In 1998 Morwood made his own find—stone tools that modern dating methods indicated were 840,000 years old. Some scientists were not convinced that Morwood had found tools. They thought that he had found tool-like natural stones. But Morwood was positive that they were tools. On the basis of his presentation, the Australian Research Council agreed to support further study on Flores.

At the end of the digging season in 2000, Morwood and his colleagues decided to look next at Liang Bua. Radien Soejono, who had led digs there in the past, was now the head of the Indonesian Centre for Archaeology in Jakarta. Morwood contacted him. Soejono was delighted to learn about new plans for Liang Bua. Although he no longer wished to do fieldwork himself, he was happy to supervise the center's team of younger scientists. A formal memorandum from the center gave the Australians permission to excavate, and in 2001, the dig at Liang Bua began. In 2003, as the dry season was ending, the first little skeleton was unearthed. The path that had begun on a hunch more than a hundred years earlier had zigzagged its way to the most incredible find of our time.

CHAPTER FOUR

THE EBU GOGO

On Flores Island, people tell their children stories about the *ebu gogo*, the small wild people who once lived outside their villages. They were very hairy, their ears stuck out, they had potbellies, and their arms were very long. They would come to the homesteads and fields and stand in clusters of two or three, watching the people and murmuring to one another.

Some villagers tried to speak to them, but they would only repeat back the words that had been spoken. If someone offered them food, for example, and said, "This is for you," they would say, "This is for you," in response.

They also caused trouble for the villagers. They stole things—crops and, sometimes, animals. The villagers thought that if they could befriend the little people, they would stop stealing. So they arranged a feast and invited the ebu gogo to join them.

The villagers built a bonfire and began to cook meat on it, but the ebu gogo seemed frightened and would not go near the fire. The villagers filled plates with food and brought the plates to their guests. The ebu gogo snatched up the food, but they threw the plates on the ground.

This was an insult, and a fight broke out. Several of the ebu gogo were killed, and the rest fled to their cave. The way there was too steep for the villagers to follow, and so the affair ended.

Villagers on Flores Island gather in Liang Bua cave. Stories of a little people known as the ebu gogo have been part of local village lore for generations.

But soon the ebu gogo resumed their raids on the villagers' crops and animals, and the villagers became more and more angry. Finally, the ebu gogo stole a baby. The villagers decided to put an end to them once and for all.

Pretending to be making another gesture of friendship, they took long bamboo poles and bales of grass and climbed as near to the cave as they could. Then, raising the bales of grass onto the poles, they passed them up to the little people, who took them eagerly. But inside the last bale, the villagers had hidden smoldering coals. A few minutes after it was taken into the cave, it burst into flame, setting the other bales and the whole cave ablaze. All the ebu gogo were killed in the fire.

Later, a young man from the village tried to climb to the cave, but he slipped from the rocks and fell to his death. The villagers considered the cave cursed, and no one ever tried to go there again.

(THE END OF THE EBU GOGO

Gunung Ebulobo, an active volcano on the southern edge of the Soa Basin, is said to be the site of the ebu gogo cave. It is 6,900 feet (2,100 m) high, spews steam from its cone, and its slopes are covered with craggy black volcanic rocks. The hot springs that bubble up in the woods near its base are bathing pools for local children. Although the ebu gogo stories are told all over Flores, the Nage people who live in the villages near the foot of Gunung Ebulobo tell them as their own. The stories differ only slightly from village to village. In one, the ebu gogo stole a child and ate it. In another, they stole a child because they wanted it to teach them how to cook—but the child quickly outsmarted them and escaped.

The legendary small people, the ebu gogo, were said to have lived in a cave on Indonesia's Gunung Ebulobo.

All the versions recount the fire in the cave, though they differ in how it was arranged and how it ended. In one, the villagers offered not bales of grass but clothing. They soaked the last bundle in cooking oil and ignited it just as they passed it up to the cave. In one version, one of the little people was seen escaping from the cave and running away. In another, two were seen to flee.

The resemblance of the ebu gogo to the little people of Liang Bua is striking. The similarities cannot be denied, but there is no proof of a connection between them. And although it is difficult to dismiss them as coincidental, that may be the explanation.

It is also possible that it is not a coincidence. Fossil evidence shows that modern human beings were on nearby islands while the little people were on Flores. Suppose—though there is no physical record of this—that the modern humans reached Flores as well. If they did, they would have come into contact with the little Floresiens, and those encounters might be the basis for the folktales. The stories might reflect events that happened perhaps thirteen thousand years ago and were passed down through the generations.

Such an unimaginably long passage of time may seem as unlikely as pure coincidence. There is a third possibility. Suppose *Homo floresiensis* did not become extinct twelve thousand years ago. Suppose they survived the geological disturbances of that time and continued to live on Flores even after modern humans arrived and settled there. Suppose they lived on the island until they were killed off by villagers, and that this happened at the time the stories say it did, between two and three hundred years ago.

(FOLKLORE STUDIES

Students of folklore have observed that certain elements, when they appear in a folktale character, often indicate that the character has a basis in reality. One such element is the amount of detail with which the character is described. Another is the absence of fantastic or magical powers. Both elements are true of the ebu gogo. They are described in great detail. And unlike similar creatures who are clearly imaginary—for example, Hawaii's little people, the *menehunes*, who arrived on the island on shooting stars—the ebu gogo don't have special powers. They don't do anything amazing and are not at all heroic. They steal food, they run away, and they are easy to fool.

Gregory Forth first heard stories about the ebu gogo of Flores Island in the 1980s.

Gregory Forth has spent years studying folklore about wild people around the world, and he has studied the Nage people and their folklore extensively. The Nage have a special category for creatures that are supernatural, and the ebu gogo are not in it. The people consider the ebu gogo to be part of history and the stories descriptions of things that really happened.

In the 1980s, when Forth first heard the stories, it "crossed his mind" that they might represent "some kind of pre-sapiens hominid that survived until just a few hundred years ago." But, as he wrote in an article for *Anthropology Today*, similar stories are found throughout the islands of Indonesia, making the possibility less likely. Because of the Liang Bua discoveries, however, Forth now believes "the possibility that they represent a real animal should be taken seriously." He says the question of whether or not that "real animal" was *Homo floresiensis* is "worth further investigation." As another researcher noted, the ebu gogo don't sound much like hobbits, but "they do sound very much like small-brained hominids trying to cope in a habitat being claimed by modern humans." According to Forth's studies of the Nage people, including family histories, he estimates that "their extermination of ebu gogo would have taken place between 1750 and 1820."

In the 1990s, anthropologist and historian Caty Husbands was told the story of the ebu gogo after she overheard an adult tease a group of children. He warned them that if they didn't go off to bed, ebu gogo would get them. She asked the man what *ebu gogo* meant. He explained that it was something they told children "to scare them." But when Husbands described the English "boogie monster," which she thought was similar, he said it was not the same. "He claimed," Husbands reported, "that ebu gogo had actually once lived just outside that very village. He insisted the story was true, and he sent me to one of the elders so I could hear more."

Husbands found it fascinating, especially the villagers' "adamant insistence" that it was true. But though her curiosity was aroused, it seemed it would not be satisfied. The villagers said they knew where the cave was, but they were not willing to go there, and it didn't seem likely that anyone ever would.

(OTHER EBU GOGO TALES

Geologist Gert van den Bergh, a member of the Liang Bua team, had also heard the stories years earlier while making a study of the terrain of Flores. At the time, the stories reminded him of leprechauns and brownies. The ebu gogo seemed a bit less fanciful, however, and the local people, he recalled, talked about them "as if they were an actual part of the fauna." After the finds at Liang Bua, he told Bert Roberts about the stories, and the two men drove together to interview the villagers.

"The tales contained the most fabulous details," Roberts later told a reporter, "so detailed that you'd imagine there had to be a grain of truth in them." It seemed odd that the ebu gogo were never described as having tools of any kind. But "some of the anatomical features sounded remarkably like *Homo floresiensis.*" The absence of tools, Roberts said, was "the only inconsistency with the Liang Bua evidence."

Bert Roberts (left), *Kira Westaway* (center), *and Chris Turney* (right) *display artist Peter Schouten's life-size drawing of the little person whose bones were found in Liang Bua.*

The stories are very specific about what the little people looked like, how they behaved, and what became of them. They are also specific about when they were killed. The people in the village closest to Gunung Ebulobo claim they were last seen in the early nineteenth century. Perhaps, Roberts says, the little Floresiens were not wiped out by the geologic disturbances twelve thousand years ago. Although they seem not to have used Liang Bua after that time, they "could well have persisted much later in other parts of the island."

Roberts's colleague Peter Brown agrees that there may be "some basis" for believing in a connection between the little Floresiens and the folktales, but he is doubtful. No remains of ebu gogo have been found, and there is no scientifically documented evidence of their existence. He said he "would be surprised" if there really was a connection. "I just think human beings have amazing imaginations and create all sorts of explanations for things which they half-see or maybe see."

Caty Husbands neatly summed up the possibilities, assuming the similarities between *Homo floresiensis* and the ebu gogo are not purely coincidental. If the scientists are correct, she said, and *Homo floresiensis* became extinct about twelve thousand years ago, then the stories must have originated at that time and "illustrate the power of oral history and collective memory." They must have been repeated to each new generation and become part of a storytelling tradition that continues to this day. "But if the scientists are wrong," Husbands went on, "and my . . . informants are correct, these creatures lived alongside the human population much more recently."

No conclusions can be drawn about the ebu gogo stories now. The fact that a tiny species really existed on an island where folktales tell of tiny creatures may only show how peculiar coincidence can be.

Or perhaps they show that human beings can pass on stories for tens of thousands of years and that stories told today as fantasy may be based on prehistoric realities. Or the folktales may show that the little human species brand new to science was quite well known to the Nage people of Flores Island until the eighteenth or nineteenth century, when the villagers tried to kill them off.

One of these three must be the correct explanation. And no matter which is true, the ebu gogo stories show us how strange reality can be and sometimes is.

CHAPTER FIVE

LITTLE CREATURES AROUND THE WORLD

According to folklore, little people are everywhere. They are often described as helpful to the big people among whom they live. In Russia, for example, stories are told about *domovoi*, friendly, hairy, little men who protect the household. Some are only 1 foot (0.3 m) tall. They help with chores, and to thank them, families may leave them treats at night. Their favorite is salted bread wrapped in a white cloth. When troubles are coming, they moan or howl in warning. When domovoi weep, there will soon be a death.

Brownies are said to live in people's homes in England and Scotland, sometimes under the stove. They are tiny but not invisible, though they prefer to be unseen and work only at night. They enjoy small gifts of food but are offended by gifts of clothing, even when theirs is shabby. Some brownies do not have noses.

In Philippine folktales, *dwende* are little people who live in human homes or in trees. They are good to families when families are good to them, and they appreciate gifts of food, which should be left on the floor.

Leprechauns are tiny men and women said to live in Ireland. Although at one time, they were helpful to human beings, they are now cranky and bad tempered and enjoy playing tricks on humans. Sometimes they hide things people are looking for, and sometimes they turn good milk sour, just for fun. They often speak in poetry.

The small people of Ireland, leprechauns, enjoy playing tricks on humans. In this illustration, they are leading a traveler astray.

Stories about gnomes are heard throughout Scandinavia and Iceland. They are said to be only about 6 inches (15 cm) tall, but they are seven times stronger than human beings and can run at speeds of 35 miles (56 km) an hour. Males wear peaked red caps, belted blue pants, and wooden shoes. Females wear peaked green caps, gray clothing, and high-topped shoes. Most gnomes stay in forests and have hardly any contact with human beings. But some, called house gnomes, live with people and can speak their language. Garden gnomes live in old gardens and enjoy telling sad stories. All gnomes are vegetarian, and they never worry.

YETIS, YOWIES, BIGFOOT: TALES OF LARGER WILD CREATURES

"In the mountains themselves live a wild people," a visitor to central Asia wrote in his journal in 1420. "A pelt covers their entire body . . . [and] they run around in the hills like animals." He could not "put a name" to them, but his account is considered the first written reference to creatures local people call Almas, which means "wildmen." They are part of the folklore of the region, and stories said to be eyewitness accounts describe them as communicating with human beings by means of gestures. Many supposed sightings were reported in the nineteenth and twentieth centures.

Similar creatures are said to have been seen around the world. People in the Himalayas tell stories about the yeti, also called the Abominable Snowman. There have been many reported sightings. On Mount Everest, a photographer from Britain's Royal Geographical Society said he spotted what looked "exactly like a human being, walking upright." He could not get a picture of it, but he was later able to photograph what he thought were its enormous footprints in the snow. Sir Edmund Hillary, the first person on record to reach the summit of Mount Everest, also reported seeing giant footprints in the snow. Australia has yowies *(right)*, described in Aboriginal folklore and said to have been sighted

by hundreds—and by some counts, thousands—of people since the first Europeans arrived. In Africa huge wild creatures variously called Chemoset, Sabrooko, Ikimizi, and other names have been reported. South Americans tell of giant creatures called Maricoxi. And North America has stories of Sasquatch ("wild man" in the Native American language of the Salish people), also called Bigfoot.

Eyewitness accounts of Sasquatch began in the nineteenth century, with the arrival of traders and miners to the Pacific Northwest. Native American folktales about them go back much further. Sightings were reported throughout the nineteenth and twentieth centuries and are still being reported today. Photographs have been taken, moving images have been captured on film, and casts of footprints have been made and studied. But none of these has been confirmed by scientists as authentic, and in the twentieth century, there were many pranks and hoaxes. Bigfoot was well known but mostly as a fake.

Some scientists are interested in Bigfoot, despite its reputation. The possibility that it might exist is being studied at the Texas Bigfoot Research Center, created in the late 1990s. The center's stated goal is "to validate what we believe to be an undocumented species of bipedal [two-legged], nocturnal [night-roaming] primate." And the Bigfoot Field Researchers Organization, a network for people who claim to have seen Bigfoot, has three thousand people in its registry.

This house gnome makes himself at home in a Swedish kitchen.

Gnomes, domovoi, brownies, leprechauns, dwende—stories about creatures like these, small and humanlike but not quite human, are found everywhere on Earth. They are clearly fanciful—from the gnomes who like to tell sad tales to the brownies who are insulted by gifts of clothing. But perhaps they are based on something real, encounters between modern human beings and other human species that were small, like *Homo floresiensis.* Perhaps small species have existed everywhere and have been known to people around the world.

Henry Gee wrote that the discovery of *Homo floresiensis,* who survived until so recently in geologic terms, "makes it more likely that stories of other mythical, humanlike creatures are founded on grains of truth." Fairy tales and folktales have been passed down for so long no one knows who first told them or why. They could be, he wrote in his book, *The Science of Middle Earth,* "poorly preserved accounts of events we no longer remember or understand."

"This is amazing stuff," columnist David Aaronovitch wrote when the finds at Liang Bua were first made public. But he found "equally amazing" some of the things people made of them, especially the idea that the worldwide folklore about small folk might be based on real creatures. Aaronovitch wrote that this suggestion "underestimates" our powers of intellect and imagination. He agreed that all human beings tell stories about little people. But, he wrote, this "speaks to something about our psyches [minds] rather than our experiences with dwarves." We tell stories about little people because we like them, and we want to be living in a world in which they exist or have existed. Children play with dollhouses and miniature cars. Adults imagine small worlds and little unseen creatures. They imagine them so deeply, they almost believe little creatures are or were real. Aaronovitch says that to think that the Liang Bua discoveries support these beliefs only shows us how strong our desires and our powers of imagination really are.

Perhaps the issue is best left to the writers of fiction who set their stories in the days of the earliest humans on Earth. Until the discoveries at Liang Bua, most such plots involved the interactions between modern human beings and Neanderthals during the time they coexisted on the European continent. Now the writers have another setting, a more recent time, and a more primitive species to imagine and suppose about.

It is also possible, however, that we will be able to go beyond fiction someday. Paleontology is a young science making enormous strides. New discoveries and new technologies are greatly adding to what we know about our species and the connections we have with others. Perhaps someday we will know enough about our earliest ancestors to compare the truth with fiction and see which is stranger.

CHAPTER SIX

LOSING THE BONES

The first little skeleton to be unearthed at Liang Bua had lain beneath the cave floor undisturbed for about eighteen thousand years. The passing millennia had covered it but not harmed it, and the person whose remains they were had probably died a peaceful death. No bones were broken, and none had been cracked, punctured, or scraped.

Thomas Sutikna, in charge of the site when the bones were discovered, made their safety and protection his first priority. Delicate and irreplaceable, they were handled with care at every stage. The seven finds that followed were treated with the same care and expertise. All were delivered unharmed to the laboratory of the Indonesian Centre for Archaeology in Jakarta, where the researchers had agreed they would be housed and studied.

But a few weeks after the discoveries were made public, the bones were removed and the discovery team was barred from seeing them. First, the skeleton of the thirty-year-old woman was taken. It was brought to the laboratory of Indonesia's foremost paleontologist, Teuku Jacob, at Mahja Gada University in Yogyakarta, almost 300 miles (500 km) away. A few days later, Jacob went to Jakarta himself and took the rest.

Professor Teuku Jacob is Indonesia's foremost paleontologist. Here he appears with a collection of normal-sized Homo erectus *fossils from Java.*

Jacob had acted with the approval of Radien Soejono, to the dismay of everyone else. He and Soejono had been colleagues for decades. They were the elder statesmen of Indonesian paleontology. As young men during World War II and after, both became national heroes—Jacob for his resistance to the Japanese occupation during the war and Soejono for his resistance to the Dutch, who continued to claim Indonesia as a colony after the war.

Jacob had been critical of the finds as soon as they were made public. He suggested that the discovery team had jumped to conclusions and that the remains were most likely just those of Pygmies, modern humans of small size. His criticism had not been given much weight, since he had not been involved in the discovery or the examinations that followed. But the criticism disturbed Soejono, and he agreed to let Jacob conduct his own examination in his own laboratory.

The center's director, Tony Djubiantono, had not been consulted. He made a series of phone calls in an attempt to have the bones returned. "Professor Jacob is a very senior person here," he said. "This makes things difficult." The other researchers were devastated.

"Professor Jacob was not part of the excavation team," Peter Brown told ABC Australia. "He had no connection at all," he said, calling Jacob's removal of the bones "bizarre." When asked what he thought would happen next, Brown could only wonder. "It's an Indonesian problem," he said. "It's something for them to resolve." He hoped the Jakarta Center would be able to get the bones back. "But," he added, "I don't think the prognosis [outlook] is good."

"We thought we would never see them again," Michael Morwood told *Nature*.

Soejono was upset by the criticism of his actions and disheartened by the anger of some of his students. He tried to be reassuring and defended his support of Jacob. "We are good friends," he said to an interviewer. "I trust him." But most people believed there was reason to be alarmed.

Although Jacob was highly respected as a leading paleoanthropologist, he had also long been criticized for the way he controlled the important fossil collection housed at his university. An article in *Science* published years before the Flores find described Jacob as "the undisputed king of paleoanthropology" in Indonesia. It also noted, however, the many complaints from scientists around the world that the important collection he controlled was "locked away" and unavailable for study.

In the article, Jacob had defended his role as a gatekeeper. He said he didn't think everyone who wanted access to the collection should have it. "We want people for whom anthropology is their life," he told the interviewer, "not just people interested in famous fossils." He was as protective of his country as he had been when it was a colony, and he made it clear that patriotism was as important to him as science. People who wished to study the fossils, he said, "have to be interested in the country," and it was clear to him that most foreign researchers were not. He considered them to be exploiting Indonesia, wishing to use the fossils found there for their own benefit, not Indonesia's.

(JACOB'S REPORT

A few weeks after Jacob took possession of the Liang Bua bones, he presented his side of the story and his "preliminary conclusions" about the find in a leading Indonesian newspaper. The article was titled, "Conflict from Flores: Storm in a Teacup."

Jacob explained why he disagreed with the analysis of the original research team, and he dismissed their claim to have discovered a new species. "The dentition [teeth]," he wrote, "clearly shows that the specimen belongs to *Homo sapiens*." The skull was so small, he explained, because the person had suffered from a genetic disease, microcephaly, which stunts the growth of the brain and skull, resulting in severe retardation and other defects. This, he thought, was what gave it "a passing resemblance to *Homo erectus*" and other premodern human skulls. But it was in fact the skull of a modern human being, a Pygmy with a brain disease.

Amanda, aged ten months, suffers from microcephaly. Some scientists suggested that the small-brained being found in Liang Bua was the result of microcephaly.

Jacob also said his analysis showed the cranial capacity to be larger "than what had been announced," and the height of the individual to be greater. But he made it clear that his concerns were about more than the discovery team's claims. He did not mention the Indonesian scientists on the team, but he was suspicious of and angry with the Australian researchers. His possession of the bones seemed to be a matter of national pride.

Since taking them, he wrote, he had been "barraged" by foreign journalists, "especially Australians." They wanted to know why he had taken the bones, when they would be returned, and why he wouldn't let the other scientists see them. One reporter had asked whether there was a turf war going on between scientists. But, he said, "threats and intimidations, even bribery and pressure, will not make our Yogyakarta team budge." The Australian government had funded much of the discovery team's work but, Jacob wrote, "research funding does not entitle that the donors may put their noses into the internal affairs of a country." The Australians, he wrote, had no right to ask that the bones be returned to the center or to see them. "There is no 'deputy sheriff' of archaeology for Southeast Asia that can push people around."

Jacob also accused Australian archaeologists of coming to Indonesia because "archaeological digs are prohibited in Australia." He perhaps was referring to the Australian prohibition against digging on land sacred to Aborigines, the continent's first inhabitants, though he did not make this clear. He regretted the fact that very few Indonesians pursue careers in archaeology. He noted, though, that many Australians do, and since they cannot dig on their own land, they "are forced to wander off to Southeast Asia."

Instead of a turf war between scientists, he suggested that what was happening could be seen as "a turf-conquest by latter-day conquistadors." He was comparing the Australian scientists to the Portuguese and Dutch colonialists who had once ruled over Indonesia. He quoted one of his supporters, who called the Australians "cultural adventurers" and concluded, "Our people should be in control of the material."

Nevertheless, Jacob concluded, he would return the bones when he was finished studying them. The whole affair had been "blown out of proportion" and amounted to nothing more than "a storm in a teacup."

Jacob kept the remains for almost four months, despite repeated requests for their return. He invited selected scientists, including Maciej Henneberg from the University of Adelaide, Australia, and Alan Thorne from Australian National University to join in the examination. They were criticized for participating, considering the conditions under which Jacob possessed the remains, but they maintained that it was not unethical for them to do so. Jacob also provided a bone fragment to the Max Planck Institute in Germany for possible DNA analysis. This violated a 1999 agreement among twenty countries, including Indonesia and Germany, not to transfer early hominid remains from one country to another. Jacob and his colleagues were criticized for this as well and for not presenting their findings in a peer-reviewed journal like *Nature*, where evidence and claims are studied by scientists before being accepted for publication. But they were confident of the correctness of their procedures and their analysis.

In January 2004, they explained their conclusions to an interviewer from the *Guardian*. The eighteen-thousand-year-old skeleton, they claimed, was that of a man, not a woman. And, as Jacob had suspected from the beginning, he had not been a member of a new species. "It's just human," he said, a modern Pygmy with microcephaly. Alan Thorne was as emphatic. He said it was "crystal clear, no shades of gray at all. It's a modern human, [though] one with many problems." He described the discovery team's conclusion as a "big mistake."

Jacob criticized *Nature*, which had published the original studies of *Homo floresiensis*. He said the journal's reviewers had been "one-sided," and he accused the Australians of having been "careless and a bit hasty." He dismissed Soejono's role, saying he "doubted" that Soejono had even read the articles, though he was listed as an author. Jacob said the younger Indonesian scientists were simply being loyal to the Australians because Australian money had funded the project. "In the present climate it's hard to get a job," he remarked. "You follow the hand that feeds you."

He explained his belief that somewhere on Flores there were living Pygmies who were descendants of the Liang Bua people. He planned to search for them. "I would say to the Australians," Jacob concluded, "do some more work. Think twice. Look at everything from different angles."

(THE BONES ARE RETURNED

The remains, with the exception of two leg bones, were finally returned on February 23, 2004. But this story does not have a happy ending. The pelvis of the little skeleton was smashed to pieces. Details that would have revealed body shape and gait were completely destroyed. The skull was badly damaged and so was one of the jawbones. "Most of the damage," said Indonesian Center director Djubiantono, "resulted from improper techniques in making molds."

Much of the detail at the base of the little skull was gone, and it was scratched. The outer part of the left eye socket had been

A fossil hominid skull is removed from a plaster cast. Then the cast of the skull is used to make accurate models of the original fossil. The Flores Island remains may have been too fragile to stand up to the mold-making process.

broken and glued back together. Two teeth had been broken off and glued back in. Bits of molded rubber were found on some sections. There were breaks in the jawbone and long, deep cut marks on both sides of the lower edge of one jawbone. The other jawbone had been broken and badly glued back together at the wrong angle. "It's sickening," Michael Morwood said.

"Breaking the Hobbit" was the headline in *Science Now*, which ran a story soon after the bones were returned. It repeated the observations that the pelvis might have been smashed during transport and that the other damage had been caused by attempts to make molds. But it also quoted Henneberg in defense of Jacob: "Professor Jacob's laboratory has decades of experience caring for fossils," he said, "and I would be surprised to learn that if they made a mold it would damage the bones."

Renowned paleontologist Tim White of the University of California at Berkeley—one of the discoverers of Lucy, the best-known australopithecine skeleton—explained what he thought had happened. Although making a mold is usually an excellent way to study fossil skulls, he said, it is not a method that can be used on wet fossils. The first little skeleton had been water-logged when it was discovered. Even when it was dry, he recalled, "the remains were seen as too fragile to ever mold by the discovery team." It was for this reason that Brown had taken CT scans of the skull before the bones were removed by Jacob.

Jacob later told *Science* that he had made molds and casts, but that it was "impossible" for the procedures done in his laboratory to have harmed the bones. "If breakage took place," he stated, "it must have happened during transport." Instead of damaging the bones, he said, he and his colleagues had worked on their reconstruction. "We tried to improve some of the things," Jacob stated. "We didn't damage any bones. Actually, we improved some."

CHAPTER SEVEN

THE INVESTIGATION

Letters of protest were circulated and petitions drawn up in criticism of Jacob and the scientists who had examined the bones with him. Jacob denied that accepted scientific rules had been broken and that he was responsible for damaging the remains. But no one could deny that the damage was serious. Hard feelings continued all around.

"It's an outrage," Peter Brown said in an interview. "The pelvis was whole; now it is 100 crumbs."

"Putting aside our own egos," Bert Roberts said, the "irretrievable" damage was "tragic for science."

Tim White said it was "clear" to him "that the Indonesian government should appoint a neutral fact-finding body to fully investigate."

Nevertheless, the focus of the discovery team soon returned to the fossils themselves. "Now she [the female skeleton] and her fellow fossils are back home," one reporter noted, "the investigation can continue."

(THE TOOLMAKER

The most baffling issue for the scientists was the intelligence of the little people. It didn't seem possible, with their grapefruit-sized

Chris Stringer of the Natural History Museum in London points out the fossil skull that was found in Liang Bua. The brain this skull contained was only the size of a grapefruit.

Australian anthropologist Peter Brown was one of the lead members of the team that excavated Liang Bua.

skulls and tiny brains, that they had been intelligent enough to make the fine tools found in the cave with them.

Peter Brown had acknowledged early on that it was difficult to believe. The tools found at Liang Bua, he wrote, are "unlike anything ever made by *Homo erectus* or any other early human species," and "just like those made by *Homo sapiens* on various parts of the planet." In his view, there were three possibilities, as he explained to an interviewer from *Scientific American.* "Either *Homo sapiens* . . . [were] making these stone tools; or this small hominid learned to make the stone tools from *Homo sapiens* in some way; or it was actually making the tools itself."

But the oldest tools had been made forty thousand years before *Homo sapiens* are known to have arrived in the area. No *Homo sapiens* remains had been found with any of the tools, even those that were more recent. Thus, there was little likelihood and no evidence at all that they had been there when the tools were made. But there was evidence that the little people had been there. Brown thought it most reasonable, therefore, to conclude that the little people "were the ones who made the tools."

Michael Morwood had also acknowledged the contradiction. The artifacts just seemed "too sophisticated" to have been made by a creature with such a small brain. But he too noted that the evidence pointed to them and that there was "no evidence for modern humans at the site at the time."

In a panel discussion with Brown and Morwood, biological anthropologist Colin Groves explained his belief that the tools themselves were evidence of the presence of *Homo sapiens*. "My suggestion," he said, "is that in fact *Homo sapiens* was making these tools, and either hunting the hobbits or coexisting with them." This would mean that *Homo sapiens* had reached Southeast Asia many thousands of years earlier than scientists believed, but it was possible. There were many ways to account for the absence of *Homo sapiens* remains—perhaps the little people had stolen the tools—and no one could deny that some remains might be found in the future.

"Maybe something will turn up at Liang Bua in the end," Brown acknowledged, although he strongly believed that the toolmaker was *Homo floresiensis*. The "association" between the tools and the little skeletal remains, he said, "seems fairly clear."

(BRAIN STUDIES

In March the association became clearer. Studies of the little brain had been conducted by a team of scientists working under Dean Falk of Florida State University. Falk was a paleoneurologist and a

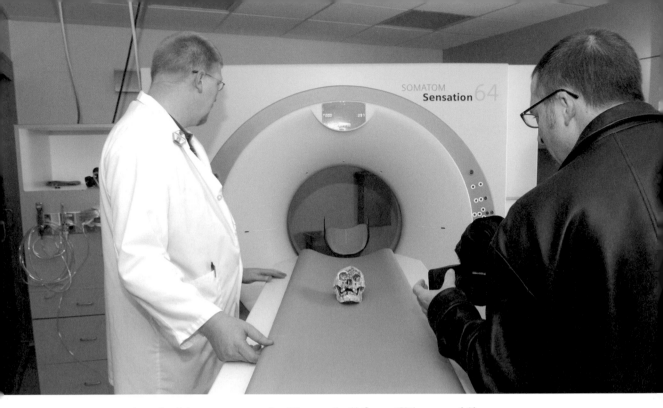

A technician prepares the Flores skull for a CT scan while a photographer captures the event on film.

pioneer in the use of CT scans to study ancient skulls. It was to her that Brown had sent the scans he made when he realized the skull was too delicate for molding. The team, made up of American, Indonesian, and Australian scientists, including Morewood and Brown, could not study the brain itself, but the CT scans and other new technologies enabled them to study how it functioned.

At the Mallinckrodt Institute of Radiology in Saint Louis, Missouri, Falk and her colleagues used the scans and computer software to construct a three-dimensional map of the space where the brain used to be. This "virtual" brain, from which a latex mold and plaster cast were later modeled, showed everything, down to the smallest details. These included the way the brain tissues had folded, for example, and where blood vessels had been located. And it showed, as one science writer put it, that "this little creature packed some very advanced features into its very small skull."

"It's remarkable," said anthropologist Charles Hildebolt, a member of Falk's team. "We've always been taught and

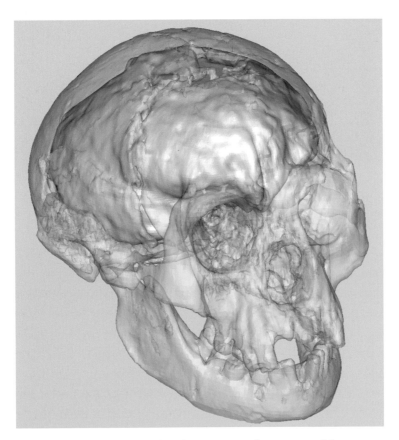

Using CT scanning technology, researchers were able to put together a representation of the size and shape of the Flores brain (highlighted) relative to its skull in this computer-generated image.

Researchers Dean Falk (left), Charles Hildebolt (center), and Kirk Smith use equipment at the Mallinckrodt Institute of Radiology to find out more about the hobbit's brain.

thought that as humans evolved, the bigger the brain, the better they are." But this chimp-sized brain had had large temporal lobes, which are associated with hearing and understanding speech. And it had very convoluted, or deeply folded, frontal lobes. (The folds enable the brain to fit more brain tissue in a small area.) The frontal lobes are active in higher forms of reasoning—planning for the future, for example, and figuring out how to solve problems, rather than proceeding by trial and error. The brain was both remarkably small and remarkably complicated. The creature who possessed it could certainly have made the stone tools and more.

Many scientists continued to find the combination of small brains and high intelligence too problematic to accept. Even

Chris Stringer was reluctant to conclude that the little people had made the sophisticated tools. He remained "cautious," he said, "about drawing too many conclusions" concerning brain quality and what the Floresiens might or might not have been able to do. An article in *Scientific American* suggested that the full-size ancestors of *Homo floresiensis* might have originally created the tools. Perhaps as they became smaller, they became incapable of such inventions but could copy what already existed.

"The matter is far from settled," Bert Roberts said. But he was willing to express a cautious conclusion. "It would appear," he told an interviewer, "based on this study, that our intelligence is defined more by the way the brain is wired than it is by sheer size." He also acknowledged that until we have a "better grip" on what the "hobbits" could and could not do, it would remain an open question.

Other scientists were less restrained. "The real take-home message," wrote one, "is that advanced behaviors . . . do not necessarily require a large brain." Henry Gee of *Nature* was even more emphatic. "The whole idea that you need a particular brain size to do anything intelligent is blown away by this find," he wrote.

⟨ A PLACE ON THE FAMILY TREE

The Falk team also concluded that the little people were a new species and helped in the search for their place on the family tree. They compared the virtual brain they had created with casts of the brains of other creatures. These included early human ancestors from three million years ago; *Homo erectus*, from two hundred thousand years ago; gorillas and chimpanzees; and modern human beings, including one adult African Pygmy and one adult who had suffered from microcephaly. The little brain was not exactly like any of them. It seemed to be unique, a species of its own.

Falk recalled that they had expected the brain to most closely resemble the chimpanzee's brain, but instead "it was more like that of bigger creatures." In its overall shape, it was most similar to the brain of *Homo erectus*. But it was not simply a miniature version. For one thing, it was much smaller than the brain of a scaled-down *Homo erectus* would have been. Even more important, in some ways, it was more primitive than *Homo erectus* and more like even earlier hominids. For example, it had a very small occipital lobe, the part of the brain that processes visual information. And in other ways, most notably in the complex frontal lobes, it was much more advanced and more like *Homo sapiens*.

As Michael Morwood put it, the little brain was "a really strange combination of some very advanced traits, some that are very primitive, and some that are unique." Peter Brown said it was like a "grab bag of hominid spare parts."

The brain study could determine nothing about the little people's ancestry or their relationship to other species. Morwood and others continued to believe that they were the dwarfed descendants of *Homo erectus*. But Dean Falk suggested that perhaps both species were descended from a common ancestor that branched into two while still in Africa. One group was the larger, less intelligent *Homo erectus*, whose remains have been found in many places. The other was the small, quite intelligent species whose remains had just been discovered. Perhaps the Floresiens arrived from Africa small, smart, and on their own almost two million years ago, as *Homo erectus* had.

Brown was inclined to agree with this and to go even further. Because of their strange combination of features, he said, perhaps "this lineage has greater antiquity [arose earlier]" than *Homo erectus*. Perhaps they arrived separately, just as they were, "on an earlier migration out of Africa."

Everyone agreed that more evidence was needed. It was clear to some scientists that the little brain represented a new species, but it could not be determined when or where—or how—it had originated. Examining the brain solved the puzzle of the little people's intelligence but added to the mystery of their origin.

The Falk studies did seem, however, to resolve the issues raised by Jacob concerning Pygmies and microcephaly. The Floresien's brain shared no special similarities with the brain of an adult Pygmy, which is the same in both size and shape as that of larger-bodied people. And it was not at all like the brain of a person suffering from microcephaly. For that disease, Falk observed, "it was totally the wrong shape." Microcephalic brains are smooth, for example, and pointed on top. The little brain was highly convoluted and round on top. Of all the brains with which it was compared, Charles Hildebolt reported, the one it resembled "least" was that of a microcephalic. For Chris Stringer, demonstrating that the brain was not that of a *Homo sapiens*, Pygmy, or microcephalic was "the most significant aspect" of the study.

(OTHER OPINIONS

Jacob and his associates dismissed Falk's findings. Maciej Henneberg said the study should be discounted because it considered only one of several kinds of microcephaly. The Liang Bua skull, he insisted, had not belonged to a member of a new species but to "a human being who suffered from a growth disorder."

This criticism was given some support by Ralph Holloway, a researcher at the Mallinckrodt Institute who had not

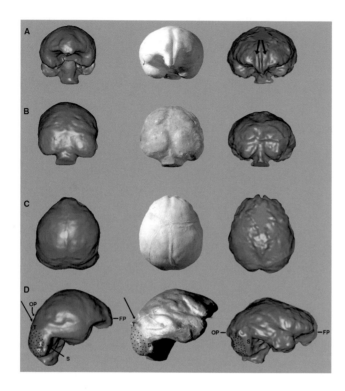

Views of two microcephalic brains (left and center) are compared with a computerized image of the cast of the brain from the skull found in Liang Bua.

participated in the study. He praised the Falk report in general and said that it made a "convincing case for ruling out pathology [sickness]." He added, though, that if the research had included a greater sample of microcephalics, its conclusions would have been stronger.

By and large, the Falk studies were accepted as authoritative, an important confirmation of the little people's uniqueness and their intelligence. It seemed that a new species had indeed been found, tiny humans who had lived on Flores Island for thousands of years before *Homo sapiens*, reached other islands in the area and who continued to live there for thousands of years after.

CHAPTER EIGHT

ENCOUNTERS TO PONDER

No proof exists at present, but many scientists believe that the little people and full-size humans met. Chris Stringer thinks they must have. Modern humans must have been on Flores while the little people were there, he says, and "must surely have encountered this tiny relative of ours." Michael Morwood also thinks "it is certain that they came face to face on occasion."

But there is no hard evidence. Although we know that modern humans were on nearby islands and on the continent of Australia by forty-five thousand years ago, there is no proof of their presence on Flores Island itself until eleven thousand years ago. Nevertheless, Bert Roberts also finds it "inconceivable" that modern humans didn't "stumble" across Flores earlier. "Surely we must have done," he says, though of course, "we need the sites and skeletons on Flores to validate this." Like Morwood, he believes they will be found and will prove that full-size and tiny humans coexisted on Flores for thousands of years.

"I don't believe it," said Jared Diamond, renowned anthropologist and prize-winning author. "My guess is that within one hundred years of modern *sapiens* arriving on the island, the dwarves would have been exterminated." In part, Diamond's belief is based on the fact that modern human beings are extremely territorial and aggressive. "We know that modern humans, given the opportunity, exterminate other modern humans," he said. "I cannot believe that they would have failed to exterminate these dwarves in a very short time."

Roberts, asked to respond to Diamond's comment, said he

thought the little people had been "fully capable of taking care of themselves" and would have been "more than a match for us." They were "the incumbents [the people already settled there] on Flores," he said. They had been living on the island for many thousands of years. And they were intelligent enough to recognize danger. After all, "they were slaying Komodo dragons and half-ton elephants." Full-size humans, on the other hand, would have arrived ignorant about the island and would have had no idea about the capabilities of these small creatures. "Who would you back in a fight to the death?" Roberts asked.

(LIVING TOGETHER IN PEACE?

Jared Diamond did not think the two groups would have shared the island peacefully. In traditional societies, he explained, strangers are always considered dangerous. When a new group moves into an area that is already occupied, a "period of negotiation" usually begins. Unless the two groups can benefit from one another in some way, they will see each other as enemies and fight to the death or until one of them leaves.

The peaceful coexistence of Pygmies and their full-size neighbors in the Congo basin is a modern example. The Pygmies and their neighbors are not uneasy with one another, Diamond said, because "they have different economies, which match." The Pygmies are hunter-gatherers, and the full-size people are farmers. They are not in competition because they don't use the same resources. Instead, each has something to offer the other, one from wild plants and wild animals, the other from cultivated fields and domesticated animals. But on Flores, both groups would have been hunter-gatherers. They would have been in competition with one another, and there

These Pygmies, who live in the Congo, pose with a tourist.

would have been no basis for trade. "We know that the arrival of *Homo sapiens* on all other islands and continents in the world was accompanied by waves of extinction and terminations," Diamond said. "How could the micropygmies [the little people] have survived the onslaught of *Homo sapiens*?" It might have taken even less than one hundred years, he said on reflection, perhaps only ten, from the time *Homo sapiens* arrived until the time the little people were exterminated.

In the end, however, even Diamond believes that the question is open. "Unless all the dates are wrong," he said, modern humans and the little people were in the same area for about thirty thousand years. He "can't conceive of a long . . . overlap," but he doesn't think the dates are wrong. "Hence," he concluded, "I don't know what to make of the reported coexistence." He supposes that it is possible, but if it did happen, he said, "it would astonish me."

"It is worth bearing in mind," Bert Roberts said, "that these are just opinions we are expressing, not matters of fact." At present there is no way to settle the matter. There is no proof that full-size *Homo sapiens* were on the island before twelve thousand years ago or that the little Floresiens were there after that time. "We can speculate endlessly," he added, but we don't have the evidence to show us "who was eating whom," or whether the two were able to avoid one another. "It'll be fascinating to see how the issue resolves itself in due course," he said. Right now, "it's back to the field, to search for more clues!"

(OTHER HUMAN SPECIES

Michael Morwood, Thomas Sutikna, Bert Roberts, and many members of the discovery team think it is likely that bands of small humans also lived on other islands. They would have been marooned there, as the Floresiens were, and evolved in ways we have yet to discover. Morwood thinks we will "almost certainly" find evidence of this. "I think we're going to have a plethora [abundance] of new human species showing up," he told an interviewer. "The history of human evolution and dispersal has clearly been more complex than previously believed."

All the islands east of Wallace's Line are promising. Many have caves and other likely sites that have never been fully explored. Roberts thinks the different islands might each have had their "own array" of creatures now extinct, including their own species of human. "Perhaps," he told an interviewer, "the far-flung Indonesian islands have acted as a series of independent Noah's Arks, each with their own trademark . . . dwarfs and giants."

New excavations in the Soa Basin have already unearthed hundreds of tools nearly a million years old. Many observers are as

Recent excavations in the Soa Basin have discovered numerous million-year-old tools.

confident as Morwood that remains of their makers, the first humans on the island and the ancestors of the little people, will also eventually be found. If they are and if they turn out to be full-size *Homo erectus*, questions about dwarfing and the island rule will be settled, but new questions will arise. The most troubling questions concern, once again, the intelligence of the little people.

If they are the dwarfed descendants of *Homo erectus*, they became not only smaller than their ancestors but smarter. This contradicts a basic assumption about human evolution—that it proceeded along a line toward larger and more capable species. A species that decreased in brain size while it increased in intelligence evolved in a way that goes against what is thought to be the general pattern of evolution itself.

Nevertheless, this may be what happened. But as everyone acknowledges, other possibilities must also be considered. If the Floresiens were small and intelligent when they arrived, as Dean Falk and Peter Brown have suggested, it would certainly be easier to understand how they got to Flores. As Roberts pointed out, "the people who made the tools could have conducted ocean crossings."

Not all the questions raised by the little people are about the past, and the search isn't only for evidence of their ancestors or other extinct species. Because they were alive so recently and coexisted in the region with modern human beings for such a long time, many believe that other bands of humans similar to the Floresiens may be alive in the world today.

"We have to entertain the possibility," says anthropologist Robert Kruszynsky, of the Natural History Museum of London, "that somewhere within the islands of Southeast Asia, early types of human beings—long thought to have been extinct—may indeed still survive." Recent discoveries in the animal world, including the 1992 discovery of a previously unknown species of ox, encourage many people to agree. "If animals as large as oxen can remain hidden in a world in which scientists seem to have rustled every tree and bush in search of new forms of life," observed *Nature*'s Henry Gee, there might be other species too, including other human species, of which we now know nothing. Creatures like the Floresiens, he wrote, might well still exist "somewhere in the unexplored tropical forests of Indonesia."

Jared Diamond smiled when he was asked for his opinion on this question. "No," he told the interviewer. "It's not possible." There is no place on our planet, he explained, where a small primitive species might continue to live today and certainly not in Indonesia. People have been "tramping around" the islands for thousands of years. Scientists—geologists, zoologists, anthropologists, archaeologists—have been exploring the terrain and digging in caves for one hundred years. "Might there be tiny people out there in the jungle?" he repeated the interviewer's question and then answered it: "No. No chance whatsoever." When pressed to name a place where he would look if he had to, he answered, "In another galaxy, certainly not on earth."

This saola, a previously unknown species of mammal, was discovered in the highlands of Vietnam in 1992. Scientists debate whether it is possible that humanlike relatives are living undiscovered in the world's remote areas.

For Roberts, the thought of finding a new species of human alive today is "stunning" and can't be dismissed as impossible, though the chances are "vanishingly small." There is a great deal more to be investigated before anyone can be completely certain of anything. He won't dismiss the possibility, no matter how remote, that "*Homo floresiensis* survives up until the present day in a remote pocket of a remote island of Southeast Asia."

The issues all depend on evidence that has yet to be found. "No amount of navel-gazing and hypothesizing," as Bert Roberts said, "can substitute for dogged fieldwork." Even the best predictions may turn out to be wrong, and the most unexpected thing may be what actually happened. Most other finds of the past twenty years could have been predicted on the basis of evidence already gathered, but not the finds at Liang Bua. Brown expressed the attitude of most scientists when he said that he would no longer predict anything, except that the future will contain "major surprises."

CHAPTER NINE

PYGMIES, PROBLEMS, AND THE CLOSING OF THE CAVE

In February 2005, even before the Falk studies of the brain were made public, Michael Morwood, Thomas Sutikna, and their team were excavating again, this time on Java. Whoever the ancestors of *Homo floresiensis* were, they would have passed through Java before reaching Flores.

The cave they were exploring, Song Gupuh (which means "flee cave") is, like Liang Bua, a limestone cave with exceedingly deep silt. They thought its deepest levels might have been laid down one hundred thousand years ago, and it was exciting to imagine what they would find if they could reach it. They planned to explore other islands as well. In June, as the monsoon rains receded, they would return to Flores, the Soa Basin, and Liang Bua.

In March the Falk report was published, and in April, Teuku Jacob headed for Flores, not to find the ancestors of the little people but to find their descendants. He continued to believe the tiny skull was not the sign of a new species but of an old disease. He was sure that the remains at Liang Bua were simply those of Pygmies. He hoped to find living Pygmies who could be shown to be related to the fossils, but he thought that finding any population of Pygmies would strengthen his claim.

In 2005 Morwood, Sutikna, and their team excavated the Song Gupuh cave on Java looking for ancestors of the little people of Flores.

(THE PYGMY CONTROVERSY

In May Jacob announced his success. The Rampasasa Pygmy Somatology Expedition, a team of physical anthropologists led by Jacob, had discovered a community of seventy-seven families living not far from Liang Bua, in which 80 percent of the people were small enough to be considered Pygmies. The expedition collected data over a period of one week. At an average height of 53 inches (1.3 m), the Rampasasa Pygmy were taller than the people of Liang Bua. But the researchers learned that they sometimes married and had children with full-size people and that their grandparents and great-grandparents had been smaller.

Jacob expressed great satisfaction with the find. The Rampasasa Pygmies, he explained, had lived in the area for longer than anyone could trace, "for hundreds or maybe even thousands of years." The discovery of their existence, he believed, demonstrated the correctness of his belief and should "shatter" the argument between himself and the Liang Bua discovery team.

His find did not, however, resolve the disagreement. Most scientists, when asked for their opinion, were skeptical. The study had not been presented in a reputable peer-reviewed journal, and the logic of the connection between the Liang Bua remains and the Rampasasa Pygmies was unclear. Most of the data had been about the villagers' small size. "You can't refute the claim that the [Liang Bua] fossils are a separate hominid species," wrote award-winning science writer Carl Zimmer, "by showing that living Pygmies on Flores are very short." He also pointed out that Jacob and his researchers "have yet to publish any of this in a scientific journal where their claims could be put to some serious scrutiny." In addition, he noted that Jacob had offered no explanation of the fact that the Liang Bua skeletons were very differently proportioned from those of modern humans, including Pygmies.

Asked for his comment, Peter Brown said that "many pockets of small-bodied people" have been found in various parts of Southeast Asia. They are, like African Pygmies, simply modern humans of small body size. "They don't have the anatomical characteristics of *Homo floresiensis*—the unique jaw, teeth, pelvis." And they don't have long arms and small brains.

A paleontologist on the original discovery team, Rukus Awe Due, said Jacob's search was "misguided." Bert Roberts said the people Jacob found were "irrelevant" to the Liang Bua controversy. The Pygmies of Rampasasa "are just diminutive modern humans," he said, "and differ from you and me only by virtue of being short."

But the controversy had gone on long enough, according to the Indonesian Institute of Sciences, a government agency whose mission is to advise the president on matters of scientific policy. In June 2005, the institute ordered Liang Bua closed to further research.

Professor Umar Jenie, chairman of the institute, explained the closing as an attempt to "prevent the dispute [from] getting worse." He suggested it would be temporary and that it had been done as an intervention. "If we don't have a cooling-down period," he said, "I worry that the relationship between Indonesian and Australian scientists will deteriorate."

The sense of the decision was not apparent. The fact that Indonesian scientists were part of the original team made it even more confusing. But there was no appealing it. Michael Morwood and all his colleagues were denied permits to return. Nevertheless the dispute continued.

CHAPTER TEN

FURTHER EVIDENCE

In October 2005, exactly one year after the discoveries were first made public and four months after the cave was ordered closed, the original team published another report in *Nature*. The earlier articles had concentrated on the one almost-complete skeleton, that of the thirty-year-old woman. Now, though the remains had been returned to them damaged, their continued examination enabled the team to present further evidence and fill out the picture.

"We can now reconstruct the body proportions of *H. floresiensis* with some certainty," the report began. The group had examined bone fragments from what turned out to be nine individuals. They had been able to estimate the height of five of them. One was a child who was five years old at death and 20 inches (51 cm) tall. The others had been adults, about 3 feet (almost 1 m) tall. The first skeleton found at Liang Bua had been "the basketball player," Peter Brown remarked; she was the tallest individual of the lot.

The bones were much thicker than those of *Homo sapiens*. The Liang Bua people would have had very heavy, strong muscles. Short though they were, "you wouldn't want to arm wrestle" one, Brown said.

Their body proportions, including their very long arms, were different not only from healthy, average *Homo sapiens* but also from exceptional and diseased *Homo sapiens*—Pygmies, dwarfs, and people suffering from microcephaly. The second jawbone was of special interest because it was direct evidence that another individual had had the same strange tooth roots and tiny skull as the first skeleton that was found and it had lived three thousand years later.

The odds against finding the remains of any member of an extinct species are extremely high. The odds against finding one that would have been an oddity, such as an individual who suffered from microcephaly, are even higher. The odds against finding two who had happened to have the same rare disease are just about inconceivable. These odds, combined with the fact that the remains spanned thousands of years, were more than enough to establish that the first little skeleton was not an exception, an oddity, or a sick individual. Instead, the report stated, it was typical, "representative of a long-term population" of small but healthy people with unique and tiny brains.

"The idea of a diseased anomaly appears to have been dealt a death blow," said one New Zealand newspaper. "You can't have a population of microcephalics going through time," Bert Roberts said in *Nature*. "That's crazy." Another paleontologist, writing in the same issue of *Nature*, put it in more scholarly language. "A population of short microcephalic humans that survived for a long time . . . or one that was susceptible to high frequencies of microcephaly and dwarfism," he wrote, "strains credulity [belief]." He concluded: "It seems reasonable for Morwood and colleagues to stick to their original hypothesis that *H. floresiensis* is a new species."

(NEW ANCESTORS

The researchers themselves had changed their thinking about another part of their hypothesis. It seemed less likely now, not only to Peter Brown but to everyone, that the little people were the descendants of *Homo erectus* and more likely that they were related to the australopithecines, Lucy's family. In body proportions and size, including brain size, they were almost identical.

Though it had always been believed that the little australopithecines never left Africa, perhaps they did. Perhaps the Floresiens were part of a migration we know nothing about. In that case, dwarfing was not the explanation of their size—their small ancestors were. And a big brain was not as important as it was thought to be in leading to the migrations of hominids around the world.

"The genealogy of *Homo floresiensis* remains uncertain," the New Zealand newspaper article concluded, but Brown had

A reconstruction of the australopithecine named Lucy is on display at the Senckenberg Museum in Frankfurt, Germany.

already begun research into the possible connection with Lucy. Nothing is "set in stone," he said. "You find new data and you adjust your position accordingly."

"I think the story of *Homo floresiensis* is going to be more complex than we originally envisaged, and more interesting," Michael Morwood added. "It's a totally unique situation and the end result seems to be also totally unique."

The report in *Nature* also described evidence suggesting that the little Floresiens had made campfires—a small pile of charred pebbles, and a set of five charred stones arranged in a circle had been found at Liang Bua. All in all, *Nature* writer Rex Dalton commented, the evidence newly presented "is likely to convince any remaining skeptics that a new species of human has been identified."

But, of course, it didn't. In the October issue of *Science*, which had presented the Falk studies six months earlier, a team of German researchers published an article disputing them. The researchers, led by neurologist Jochen Weber, had studied the brains of nineteen microcephalics and compared them with Falk's images of the brain of the little woman. They noted similarities in size—and in one case shape—and concluded that microcephaly could not be ruled out.

The Falk team, invited to respond, reported that they found it difficult to evaluate the study. They gave several reasons. First, the authors did not provide the measurements they used for their comparisons. Some of their measurements were not based on the ones usually taken to measure brains, which made them difficult to check. And in one instance, when four images were presented as different views of the same skull cast, the Falk team noted that they "could not represent the same individual." They requested that the Weber team present the findings again.

LUCY AND THE FIRST FAMILY

A little skeleton nicknamed Lucy is the best known of the australopithecines. These creatures were not human, but they walked upright and are the earliest known ancestors of human beings. Fossil evidence shows that they lived from about four million to one and a half million years ago. It is generally believed that they became extinct without ever leaving Africa. They were 3.5 to almost 5 feet (107 to 152 cm) tall and had brains about one-third the size of modern human brains.

There were several kinds of australopithecines. Some were small and slender; paleontologists call them gracile. Others, called robust, had very large teeth and heavier bones. Lucy, whose full scientific name is *Australopithecus afarensis*, was one of the smaller types.

She was discovered in 1974 in the Hadar region of Ethiopia by a young American paleoanthropologist, Donald Johanson, and a visiting graduate student from California. Johanson and his colleague, Timothy White, had organized the expedition.

On the day Lucy was found, Johanson had been planning to stay in camp doing paperwork. But he went out with the student, Tom Gray, because, as Johanson recalled, he was "feeling lucky." They spent several hours surveying the slopes of a gully. At noon, with the temperature above 100°F (38°C), they began the trek back to their jeep. But before they reached it, Johanson spotted something in the sand and the men detoured for a closer look. It turned out to be part of an arm bone. Nearby was the back of a small skull and a thighbone. There were other skeletal fragments as well. "In that 110-degree [43°C] heat we began jumping up and down," Johanson wrote, "the remains of what seemed almost certain to be parts of a single hominid skeleton lying all around us."

They returned to camp with their news, and that afternoon, everyone went to the gully. It was sectioned off, and the collection of fragments began.

"The camp was rocking with excitement," Johanson wrote. "That first night we never went to bed at all. We talked and talked." A tape recorder played a song by the Beatles, "Lucy in the Sky with Diamonds," over and over. "At some point during that unforgettable evening" the fossil picked up the name.

Two work crews had checked the gully where Lucy was found before Johanson and Gray got there. Those crews had found nothing. "Perhaps," Johanson wrote, "they had been looking in another direction. Perhaps the light was different. Sometimes one person sees things that another misses, even though he may be looking directly at them."

Johanson also realized that the remains had come to the surface only within the last year or two. If he had searched there five years earlier, they would still have been buried. Five years later, they might already have been gone, washed away by the rains.

Although other australopithecine remains were found before Lucy and some have been found since, no other skeleton as complete has ever been discovered. Lucy, at about 3.5 million years old, is the oldest, best-preserved skeleton of a human ancestor ever found.

Fragments from eight other individuals, including two infants, were later found nearby. Together with Lucy, they are known as the First Family.

Scientists around the world continue to study the evidence and debate the issues. Although Jacob said he would need to see a great many skulls in order to change his mind, Carl Zimmer noted that "just a single additional braincase would help enormously." This was echoed by almost everyone who cared to comment and makes the ban on digging, in Carl Zimmer's words, even "more incomprehensible."

Only a small part of Liang Bua, which Brown calls "the crown jewel of caves," has been excavated. "This is where the team should be focusing," he said. No one can disagree, but "my guess," said Morwood, "is that we will not work at Liang Bua again, this year or any other year."

In a better world, such a thing would never happen. Secret agendas, pride, and anger would have nothing to do with the progress of science. But in truth, they have always been a part of its history. Eugene Dubois hid his incredible find under his dining room floor for forty years. The Dead Sea Scrolls, ancient texts containing parts of the Christian Bible that were discovered in a series of caves in the 1950s, were not fully available for study until 1995.

If the past is any guide, Liang Bua will be open again someday. Scientists hope it will be open within months, not years. "The politics of science is complex," Brown said, "and the current situation can easily change." World opinion and public pressure will certainly influence the course of events.

Whenever the ban is lifted, Liang Bua will still be there. And there will be people trying to understand its story. The rest of the world will be waiting to hear.

It will be as true then as it is now that science, as Brown likes to say, will always surprise us and that everything depends on the evidence.

WHAT IS POSSIBLE?

If Eugene Dubois hadn't set out for Southeast Asia on a hunch and made one of the luckiest finds in the history of paleontology, it is entirely possible that we would never have known about Flores Island's incredible past. One of our foremost evolutionary theorists, Stephen Jay Gould, believed that reality is always like that—many things are just as possible as the thing that actually happens.

Liang Bua has been closed, but even if scientists never learn any more about the little people, the bones already discovered have shown them some of their earlier errors and pointed them in directions they would not have taken otherwise. This is a great gift. If in addition, they make all of us more careful about what we say we know and more inclined to wonder, that would be another gift as great.

And if the interest and concern of people around the world hastens the reopening of Liang Bua, the little Floresiens may yet help scientists overcome national and private interests and work together in their common human interest. That would be a gift perhaps greater than any other. We may hope that of all the futures that are possible, this is the one that comes to pass.

GLOSSARY

anomaly: something unexpected or irregular

anthropologist: a scientist who studies the development of human culture

archaeologist: a scientist who studies prehistoric human life by analyzing artifacts

artifact: something created by humans and typical of a culture

australopithecines: extinct early humanlike creatures who lived 4.4 million to 1.7 million years ago

barbs: sharply pointed objects, such as the stone tools used as spear points or arrowheads

ebu gogo: small people of legend on Flores Island

frontal lobes: the sections of the human brain active in reasoning and problem solving

Homo erectus: an early relative of modern humans who lived about 1,800,000 to 300,000 years ago. *Homo erectus* may have migrated out of Africa as early as 1,600,000 years ago.

Homo floresienses: the scientific name for the small people of Flores Island, if they prove to be a separate species

Homo neanderthalis **(Neanderthal):** a close relative of modern humans who lived about 200,000 to 30,000 years ago

Homo sapiens: modern humans who evolved about 100,000 years ago

microcephaly: a birth defect that limits the growth of the brain and skull

paleoneurologist: a scientist who studies the brains and nervous systems of ancient people

paleontologist: a scientist who studies ancient life of all kinds

Pygmies: groups of smaller than average human beings

stegodon: an elephantlike prehistoric animal

Wallace's line: an imaginary line between islands in Indonesia. Animals on one side of the line were different from those on the other side.

Source Notes

9 Michael Hopkin, "Little Lady of Flores Forces Rethink of Human Evolution," *news@nature.com*, October 27, 2004, http://www.nature.com/news/2004/041025/full/4311029a.html (March 29, 2006).

10 John Vidal, "Bones of Contention," *Guardian*, January 13, 2005, http://www.guardian.co.uk/life/feature/story/0,13026,1388500,00.html (April 6, 2006).

11 Ibid.

11 Henry Gee, "Our Not So Distant Relative," *Guardian*, October 28, 2004, http://www.guardian.co.uk/life/feature/story/0,13026,1337198,00.html (April 6, 2006).

14 Hopkin.

20 "Little People of Flores: Ask the Expert," *NOVAscienceNOW*, April 25, 2005, http://www.pbs.org/wgbh/nova/sciencenow/3209/01-ask.html (March 29, 2006).

21 "'Hobbit' Joins Human Family Tree," *BBC News: Science*, October 27, 2004, http://news.bbc.co.uk/1/hi/sci/tech/3948165.stm (March 29, 2006).

21 Kate Wong, "Digging Deeper: Q&A with Peter Brown," *Scientific American.com*, October 27, 2004, http://www.sciam.com/article.cfm?articleID=00082F87-7D35-117E-BD3583414B7F0000 (April 6, 2006).

23 M. Morwood, et al., "Archaeology and the Age of a New Hominin from Flores in Eastern Indonesia," *Nature*, October 28, 2004, 1,087–1,091.

25 Tim Radford, "From 18,000 Years Ago the One-Metre Tall Human that Challenges the History of Human Evolution," *Guardian*, October 28, 2004, http://education.guardian.co.uk/higher/research/story/0,,1337734,00.html (April 6, 2006).

25 David Aaronovitch, "Big Little man," *Guardian*, October 31, 2004, http://www.guardian.co.uk/life/science/story/0,12996,1340211,00.html (April 6, 2006).

27 Ibid.

30 Gee.

33 Michael Lemonick, "Hobbits of the South Pacific," *Time*, November 8, 2004, 52.

33 Christopher Wade, "Miniature People Add New Pieces to Evolutionary Puzzle," *New York Times*, November 9, 2004, F2.

35 Donald Johanson and Maitland Edey, *Lucy: The Beginnings of Humankind*, (New York: Simon and Schuster: 1981), 15.

41 Deborah Smith, "It's a Small World After All." *Sydney Morning Herald*, October 30, 2004, http://www.smh.com.au/news/science/its-a-small-world-after-all/2004/10/29/1099028212796.html (April 6, 2006).

42 Ibid.

49–50 Gregory Forth, "Hominids, Hairy Hominids, and the Science of Humanity," *Anthropology Today*, June 2005, 13.

49–50 Marek Kohn, "The Little Troublemaker," *New Scientist*, June 18, 2005, http://www.newscientist.com (n.d.).

50 Caty Husbands, "When Did 'Hobbit' Humans Die Out? Not So Long Ago, Say Indonesian Villagers," *Berkeley Daily Planet*, November 2, 2004, http://www.berkeleydailyplanet.com/article.cfm?archiveDate=11-02-04&storyID=20001 (April 7, 2006).

50 Ibid.

50 "Are There Hobbits in Indonesia?" *Daily News*, January 5, 2005, http://www.dailynews.co.za/index.php?fArticleId=2361742 (April 7, 2006).

50 Gee.

52 Ibid.

52 Wong.

52 Husbands.

56 "Bigfoot—Mapinguary—Sasquatch—Florida Skunk Ape—Yeti—Yowie—Other Ape-Human Creatures," Crystalinks Metaphysical and Scientific Website, n.d., http://www.crystalinks.com/bigfoot.html (April 7, 2006)

56 Ibid.

57 "Bigfoot in Texas? *Texas Bigfoot Research Center*, n.d., http://www.texasbigfoot.com (April 7, 2006).

58 Henry Gee, "Flores, God and Cryptozoology," *news@nature.com*, October 27, 2004, http://www.nature.com/news/2004/041025/pf/041025-2_pf.html (April 7, 2006).

58 Henry Gee, *The Science of Middle-earth*, (Cold Spring Harbor, NY: Cold Spring Press, 2004).

59 Aaronovitch.

62 *National Geographic News*, May 3, 2005, http://news.nationalgeographic.com/news/2005/05/0523_050523_ngm_hobbit_2.html (April 7, 2006).

62 *ABC Australia*, "Indonesian Scientist Defends His Removal of Hobbit Remains," *PM*, December 3, 2004, http://www.abc.net.au/pm/content/2004/s1257717.htm (April 7, 2006).

62 Rex Dalton, "Looking for the Ancestors," *news@nature.com*, March 24, 2005, http://www.nature.com/news/2005/050321/full/434432a.html (April 18, 2006).

63 "Hopping Mad Over Hobbits: Removal of Bones Sparks Archeological Turf War." *Sydney Morning Herald*, December 11, 2004, http://www.smh.com.au/news/World/Hopping-mad-over-hobbits-removal-of-bones-sparks-archaeological-turf-war/2004/12/10/1102625538610.html (April 18, 2006).

63 Jeffrey Mervis, "Keeper of the Keys to Fossil Kingdom," *Science*, March 6, 1998, 1,477.

63 Ibid.

63 Teuku Jacob, "Conflict from Flores: Storm in a Teacup" *Kompas*, December 2004, available online at http://accuca.conectia.es/15122004 _conflict_from_flores.htm (April 18, 2006)

64 Ibid.

65 Ibid.

65 Ibid.

65 Ibid.

65–66 Ibid.

66 Ibid.

66–67 Vidal.

67 Elizabeth Culotta, "Breaking the Hobbit," *ScienceNOW*, March 12, 2005, http://sciencenow .sciencemag.org/cgi/content/full/ 2005/323/4 (April 18, 2006).

68 "Hobbits' Triumph Tempered by Tragedy," *Sydney Morning Herald*, March 5, 2005, available online at http://www.smh.com.au/news/ Science/Hobbits-triumph-tempered -by-tragedy/2005/03/04/ 1109700677461.html (April 18, 2006)

68–69 Culotta.

69 Ibid.

69 Dan Vergano, "Fresh Scandal Over Old Bones." *USAToday.com*, March 21, 2005, http://www.usatoday .com/tech/science/discoveries/ 2005-03-21-hobbit-usat_x.htm (April 18, 2006).

69 Culotta.

71 Rex Dalton, "More Evidence for Hobbit Unearthed as Diggers Are Refused Access to Cave." *news@nature.com*, October 11, 2005, http://www.nature.com/news/ 2005/051010/full/437934a.html (April 18, 2006).

71 Vergano.

71 Ibid.

71 Richard Monastersky, "The Lady Returns." *The Economist*, March 5, 2005.

72 Wong.

73 Kohn.

73 David Keys, "Indonesia's Lost World: Shaking Up Family Tree," *Archaeology*, October 28, 2004, http://www.archaeology.org/ online/features/flores (April 18, 2006).

73 *ABC Australia*, "'Hobbit' a New Addition to Human Family," *The 7:30 Report*, October 28, 2004, http://www.abc.net.au/7.30/ content/2004/s1230212.htm (April 19, 2006).

73 Ibid.

75 Dean Falk, et al, "The Brain of LB1, *Homo floresiensis*," *Science*, March 2005.

75 Michael Balter, "Small but Smart? Flores Hominid Shows Signs of Advanced Brain," *Science*, March 4, 2005, 1,368.

75–76 Hillary Mayell, "'Hobbit'

Brains Were Small but Smart, Study Says," *National Geographic News*, March 3, 2005, http://news .nationalgeographic.com/news/ 2005/03/0303_050303_tv_hobbit .html (April 19, 2006).

77 Ibid.

77 "Little People of Flores."

77 Michael Balter, "Hobbits Get Smart." *ScienceNOW*, March 3, 2005, http://sciencenow .sciencemag.org/cgi/content/full/ 2005/303/3 (April 19, 2006).

77 "'Hobbit' Joins Human Family Tree."

78 Falk et. al.

78 Mayell.

78 Kohn.

79 Anna Salleh, "Hobbits' Long Arms Just Like Lucy's." *News in Science*, December 10, 2005, http://www .abc.net.au/science/news/stories/ s1480331.htm (April 19, 2006).

79 Balter.

79 Mayell.

79 Ibid.

79 "Tiny Human a New Species." *Discover*, March 4, 2005, http://dsc .discovery.com/news (n.d.).

80 Paul Rincon, "Hobbit Was Not a Diseased Human," *BBC News: Science*, http://news.bbc.co.uk/ 2/hi/science/nature/4308751.stm (April 19, 2006).

81 Richard Monastersky, "Meet Cousin Florence," *Economist*, October 30, 2004, 81.

81 "Ancient Tiny Humans Shed New Light on Evolution. The Flores Find: Q&A with the Scientists," *All Things Considered, National Public Radio*, October 27, 2004, http:// www.npr.org/templates/story/ story.php?storyId=4127713 (April 19, 2006)

81 "Little People of Flores."

81 Jared Diamond, interviewed by Robert Krulwich, "Little People of Flores: Jared Diamond Interview," *NOVAscienceNOW*, March 24, 2005, http://www.pbs.org/ wgbh/nova/sciencenow/3209/ 01-diamond.html (April 19, 2006).

82 "Little People of Flores."

82 Krulwich.

82 Ibid.

83 Ibid.

83 Ibid.

84 "Little People of Flores."

84 Lemonick.

84 "Ancient Tiny Humans."

85 "Little People of Flores."

86 Kohn.

86 "'Hobbit' Joins Human Family Tree."

86 Diamond, interviewed by Robert Krulwich.

87 "Little People of Flores."

87 "Mini Human Species Unearthed," *Scientific American.com*, October 27, 2004, http://www.sciam.com/article.cfm?articleID=000B7CEA-EA31-117E-AA3183414B7F0000 (April 19, 2006).

87 "The Flores Find."

90 Teuku Jacob, "The Pygmy Community of Flores." *Kompas*, May 8, 2005, available online at *The Loom weblog*, http://loom.corante.com/archives/2005/04/29/hobbits_alive.php (April 19, 2006).

90–91 Carl Zimmer, "Return to Hobbit Limbo," *The Loom weblog*, June 15, 2005, http://loom.corante.com/archives/2005/06/15/return_to_hobbit_limbo.php (April 19, 2006).

91 Jennifer Viegas, "Pygmy Village Casts Doubt on 'Hobbit' Human." *Discovery News*, May 12, 2005, http://dsc.discovery.com/news/briefs/20050509/pygmies.html (April 19, 2006).

91 Ibid.

91 Vergano.

92 M. Morwood et al. "Further Evidence for Small-Bodied Hominins from the Late Pleistocene of Flores, Indonesia." *Nature*, October 8, 2005, 1,012.

92 Salleh.

92 ABC Australia, "Hobbit Update," *Catalyst*, October 13, 2005, http://www.abc.net.au/catalyst/stories/s1481727.htm (April 19, 2006).

93 Morwood et al., "Further evidence," 1,013.

93 Francis Till, "Hobbits: A New Species of Human, Confirmed." *National Business Review* (New Zealand) October 12, 2005, http://www.nbr.co.nz/home/column_article.asp?id=13156&cid=3&cname= (April 19, 2006).

93 Dalton, "More Evidence."

93 Daniel Lieberman, "Further Fossil Finds from Flores." *Nature*, October 13, 2005, 957.

94 Till.

95 Salleh.

95 Brian Handwerk, "New 'Hobbit' Human Bones Add to Evidence, Oddity," *National Geographic News*, October 12, 2005, http://news.nationalgeographic.com/news/2005/10/1012_051012_hobbits.html (April 19, 2006).

95 Dalton, "More Evidence."

95 Jochen Weber, et al., "Comment on 'The Brain of LB1, *Homo floresiensis*,'" *Science*, October 2005, 236.

95 Falk, et al., "Response to 'Comment on "The Brain of LB1, *Homo floresiensis*,"'" *Science*, October 2005, 236.

96 Johanson and Edey, 14.

96 Ibid., 17.

97 Ibid., 18.

97 Ibid., 21–22.

98 Carl Zimmer, "Whose Brain Is It Anyway? (The Further Hobbit Adventures)," *The Loom weblog*, October 14, 2005, http://loom.corante.com/archives/2005/10/14/ whose_brain_is_it_anyway_the _further_hobbit_adventures.php (April 19, 2006).

98 Dalton, "More Evidence."

98 Ibid.

98 Peter Brown, e-mail to author, September 9, 2005.

SELECTED BIBLIOGRAPHY

BOOKS

Carroll, Sean B. *Endless Forms Most Beautiful*. New York: W. W. Norton & Company, 2005.

Diamond, Jared. *Guns, Germs, and Steel: The Fates of Human Societies*. New York: W. W. Norton & Company, 2005.

Johanson, Donald, and Maitland Edey. *Lucy: The Beginnings of Humankind*. New York: Simon and Schuster, 1981.

Larson, Edward J. *Evolution*. New York: The Modern Library, 2004.

PERIODICALS AND NEWSPAPERS

Diamond, Jared. "The Astonishing Micropygmies." *Science*, December 17, 2004.

Falk, Dean, et al. "The Brain of LB1, *Homo floresiensis*." *Science*, March 2005.

——. "Response to 'Comment on the Brain of LB1, *Homo floresiensis*.'" *Science*, October 2005.

Jacob, Teuku. "The Pygmy Community of Flores." *Kompas*, May 8, 2005.

Lemonick, Michael. "Hobbits of the South Pacific." *Time*, November 8, 2004.

Lieberman, Daniel. "Further Fossil Finds from Flores." *Nature*, October 13, 2005.

Morwood, M., et al. "Archaeology and Age of a New Hominin from Flores in Eastern Indonesia." *Nature*, October 28, 2004.

——. "Further Evidence for Small-Bodied Hominins from the Late Pleistocene of Flores, Indonesia." *Nature*, October 8, 2005.

Morwood, Mike, Thomas Sutikna, and Richard Roberts. "The People Time Forgot." *National Geographic*, April 2005.

Wade, Christopher. "Miniature People Add New Pieces to Evolutionary Puzzle." *New York Times*, November 9, 2004, F2.

Weber, Jochen, et al. "Comment on 'The Brain of LB1, *Homo floresiensis.*'" *Science*, October 2005.

WEBSITES

ABC Australia. "Hobbit Update." *Catalyst*. October 13, 2005. http://www.abc.net.au/catalyst/stories/s1481727.htm.

"Ancient Tiny Humans Shed New Light on Evolution." *All Things Considered, National Public Radio*. October 27, 2004. http://www.npr.org/templates/story/story.php?storyId=4127713 (March 29, 2006).

Balter, Michael. "Hobbits Get Smart." *ScienceNOW*. March 3, 2005. http://sciencenow.sciencemag.org/cgi/content/full/2005/303/3.

Culotta, Elizabeth. "Breaking the Hobbit." *ScienceNOW*. March 12, 2005. http://sciencenow.sciencemag.org/cgi/content/full/2005/323/4.

Dalton, Dalton, "Looking for the Ancestors," *news@nature.com*, March 24, 2005, http://www.nature.com/news/2005/050321/full/434432a.html.

Dalton, Rex. "More Evidence for Hobbits Unearthed as Diggers Are Refused Access to Cave." *news@nature.com*. October 11, 2005. http://www.nature.com/news/2005/051010/full/437934a.html.

"The Flores find." *news@nature.com*. October 2004. http://www.nature.com/news/specials/flores/index.html.

Gee, Henry. "Flores, God and Cryptozoology." *news@nature.com*. October 27, 2004. http://www.nature.com/news/2004/041025/pf/041025-2_pf.html.

———. "Our Not So Distant Relative." *Guardian*, October 28, 2004. http://www.guardian.co.uk/life/feature/story/0,13026,1337198,00.html

Handwerk, Brian. "New 'Hobbit' Human Bones Add to Evidence, Oddity." *National Geographic News*. October 10, 2005. http://news.nationalgeographic.com/news/2005/10/1012_051012_hobbits.html.

"'Hobbit' joins human family tree." *BBC News: Science*, October 27, 2004. http://news.bbc.co.uk/1/hi/sci/tech/3948165.stm.

Hopkin, Michael. "Little Lady of Flores Forces Rethink of Human Evolution." *news@nature.com*, October 27, 2004. http://www.nature.com/news/2004/041025/full/4311029a.html.

Husbands, Caty. "When Did 'Hobbit' Humans Die Out? Not So Long Ago, Say Indonesian Villagers." *Berkeley Daily Planet.* November 2, 2004. http://www.berkeleydailyplanet.com/article.cfm?archiveDate=11-02-04&storyID=20001.

Jacob, Teuku. "Conflict from Flores: Storm in a Teacup." *Kompas*, December 2004. <http://accuca.conectia.es/hobbit.htm>.

Kohn, Marek. "The Little Troublemaker." *New Scientist*, June 18, 2005. http://homepage.ntlworld.com/marek.kohn/flores.html.

Krulwich, Robert (interviewer). "Little People of Flores: Jared Diamond Interview." *NOVAscienceNOW*, March 24, 2005. http://www.pbs.org/wgbh/nova/sciencenow/3209/01-diamond.html.

"Little People of Flores: Ask the Expert." *NOVAscienceNOW*, April 25, 2005. http://www.pbs.org/wgbh/nova/sciencenow/3209/01-ask.html.

Mayell, Hillary. "'Hobbit' Brains Were Small but Smart, Study Says." *National Geographic News,* March 3, 2005. http://news.nationalgeographic.com/news/2005/03/0303_050303_tv_hobbit.html.

Radford, Tim. "From 18,000 Years Ago the One-Metre Tall Human that Challenges the History of Human Evolution." *Guardian.* October 28, 2004. http://education.guardian.co.uk/higher/research/story/0,,1337734,00.html.

Salleh, Anna. "Hobbits' Long Arms Just Like Lucy's." *News in Science.* December 10, 2005. http://www.abc.net.au/science/news/stories/s1480331.htm.

Stringer, Chris. "A Stranger from Flores." *news@nature.com*, October 27, 2004. http://www.nature.com/news/specials/flores/index.html.

"Tiny Human a New Species." *Discover.* March 4, 2005. http://dsc.discovery.com/news.

Vidal, John. "Bones of Contention." *Guardian.* January 13, 2005. http://www.guardian.co.uk/life/feature/story/0,13026,1388500,00.html.

Viegas, Jennifer. "Pygmy Village Casts Doubt on 'Hobbit' Human." *Discovery News.* 2005. http://dsc.discovery.com/news/briefs/20050509/pygmies.html.

Wong, Kate. "Digging Deeper: Q&A with Peter Brown." *Scientific American.com.* October 27, 2004. http://www.sciam.com/article.cfm?articleID=00082F87-7D35-117E-BD3583414B7F0000.

Zimmer, Carl. "Return to Hobbit Limbo." *The Loom weblog*. June 15, 2005. http://loom.corante.com/archives/2005/06/15/return_to_hobbit_limbo.php.

——. "Whose Brain Is It Anyway? (The Further Hobbit Adventures)," *The Loom weblog*. October 14, 2005. http://loom.corante.com/archives/2005/10/14/whose_brain_is_it_anyway_the_further_hobbit_adventures.php.

FURTHER READING & WEBSITES

Barnes, Trevor. *Archaeology*. Boston: Kingfisher, 2004.

BBC News
http://news.bbc.co.uk/2/hi/science/nature/4339740.stm
News about finds at archaeological digs in another area of Flores Island can be found here, with links to other news items about the little people.

Devereux, Paul. *Archaeology: The Study of Our Past*. Milwaukee: Gareth Stevens Publishing, 2002.

Jespersen, James, and Jane Fitz-Randolph. *Mummies, Dinosaurs, Moon Rocks: How We Know How Old Things Are*. New York: Atheneum Books for Young Readers, 1996.

McIntosh, Jane R. *Archaeology*. Eyewitness Books series. New York: DK, 2000.

Orna-Ornstein, John. *Archaeology: Discovering the Past*. New York: Oxford University Press, 2002.

Sloan, Christopher. *The Human Story: Our Evolution from Prehistoric Ancestors to Today*. Washington, DC: National Geographic, 2004.

Turner, Alan. *National Geographic Prehistoric Mammals*. Washington, DC: National Geographic, 2004.

Wilcox, Charlotte. *Mummies, Bones, & Body Parts*. Minneapolis: Carolrhoda Books, 2000.

Wilkinson, Phil. *Early Humans*. Eyewitness Books series. New York: DK, 2005.

Wikipedia Foundation
http://en.wikipedia.org/wiki/Flores
This site contains information on the history, geography, and culture of Flores Island.

Zuehlke, Jeffrey. *Indonesia in Pictures*. Minneapolis: Twenty-First Century Books, 2006.

INDEX

ABOUT THE AUTHOR

Linda Goldenberg is a native of Brooklyn, New York. She earned a Master's in philosophy and a Master's in Library Science. She has managed an elementary school library for more than ten years.

Goldenberg previously published under the name Linda Atkinson. She is the author of a number of award-winning books for young readers. *Kindling Flame* won the National Jewish Book Award, and *Mother Jones: the Most Dangerous Woman in America* was named a National Council for the Social Studies (NCSS)/Children's Book Council (CBC) Notable Social Studies Trade Book for Young People. *Women in the Martial Arts: A New Spirit Rising* was named to the New York Public Library Best Book for the Teenage list.

PHOTO ACKNOWLEDGMENTS

The photos in this book are used with the permission of: Chris Turney, University of Wollongong, pp. 1, 7, 8, 20, 27, 35, 45, 54, 61, 71, 81, 89, 92, 99; © Keneth Garrett, pp. 2, 6, 15, 16, 17, 44, 60, 94; © BEAWIHARTA/ Reuters/Corbis, pp. 9, 26; © SuperStock, p. 18; © Neil McAllister/Alamy, p. 23; AP/Wide World Photos, p. 24; © Dr. Justin Gerlach, p. 28; © Pascal Goetgheluck/Photo Researchers, Inc., pp. 30, 34, 68; © Hulton Archive/ Stringer/Getty Images, p. 31; © David Gifford/Photo Researchers, Inc., p. 37; © John Reader/Photo Researchers, Inc., pp. 39, 40; © Lindsay Hebberd/ CORBIS, p. 47; University of Alberta ExpressNews, p. 49; courtesy of the University of Wollongong, Australia, p. 51; © North Wind Picture Archives, p. 55; Fortean Picture Library, p. 56; Mary Evans Picture Library, p. 58; © Taro Yamasaki/Time Life Pictures/Getty Images, p. 64; © Jim Watson/ AFP/Getty Images, p. 70; © Peter Brown, p. 72; Mallinckrodt Institute of Radiology at Washington University in St. Louis, pp. 74, 75, 76; Kirk Smith, Mallinckrodt, Institute of Radiology, p. 80; © Jerry Callow/Panos Pictures, p. 83; © Sahlan Hayes/Fairfaxphotos.com, p. 85; © Masahiro Iijima/ardea.com, p. 87; © Rex Dalton, p. 88.

Cover photos: background: © Kenneth Garrett, Skull: © Peter Brown.